nF419157

Praise for
Technology Professional to Innovation Leader

"An excellent read for anyone wanting to elevate their leadership game!" **–Molly Mehner, Town Administrator, Town of Collierville, TN** "Balanced life makes better leaders and better people in general, which ties into his other challenge – for leaders to lean on their humanness (right side of the brain) to inspire their teams to innovate and achieve success."

"Not your traditional leadership book!" **–Dr. Kandi Hill-Clarke, Dean and Louise and Robert Jr. Professor, College of Education, University of Memphis.** "Madan takes the reader on a reflective journey filled with ah-ha moments, lessons learned, and practical recommendations."

"Perfect timing for this new approach to leadership development." **–Rodney McElroy, Solution Architect, HILTON.** "Leadership training that focuses on getting team members to engage in the enterprise and unleash their discretionary effort - creativity and commitment could not have come at a better time in these days of the remote worker and the quiet quitter."

"Bridges the gap between knowing and doing." **–Anuj Mehrotra, Dean, The George Washington School of Business.** "People know and can articulate the desired leadership skills and behaviors but have difficulty applying those on the job."

"Relationships are foundational." **– Wright Cox, President and CEO, BankTennessee.** "I have long believed that if you can develop good relationship skills, you can be successful in almost any field. As you state in your

book, everyone wants to feel they matter to the organization and the leader. If I truly value each employee and they feel I am willing to listen and learn from their input, they are motivated to share it. They become part of the process to success."

***"In a world of rapid change, leadership and innovation skills are more important than ever before."* - Patrick Greissing, Director Executive Research and Strategic Data, ALSAC/St. Jude.** "Madan takes the reader on a journey to distinguish exactly what it takes to enhance those skills and build relationships with individuals, at every level of an organization, to help you become the best innovation leader possible. Most importantly, he does this in a way that stresses you remain grounded in who you as a person."

***"Fresh, practical and useful"* – Vijay Govindarajan (VG),** Coxe Distinguished Professor, Tuck School of Business at Dartmouth College, and author of the Best Seller Three Box Solution. "Every technical/analytical professional can unleash their leadership potential by applying the proven ideas in this book."

Technical Professional
To
Innovation Leader

Technical Professional To Innovation Leader

A HOW-TO Guide for Unleashing Your People Leadership and Innovation Skills

Proven and practical ideas from leaders at Google, Apple, Microsoft, Amazon, Audi, Hilton, FedEx, TCS, IBM, and others

MADAN BIRLA

Author of *FedEx Delivers* and *Unleashing Creativity and Innovation*

Copyright © 2024 by Madan Birla

All rights reserved.

No portion of this book may be reproduced in any form without written permission from the publisher or author except as permitted by U.S. copyright law.

This publication is designed to provide accurate and authoritative information in regard to the subject matter covered. It is sold with the understanding that neither the author nor the publisher is engaged in rendering legal, investment, accounting or other professional services. While the publisher and author have used their best efforts in preparing this book, they make no representations or warranties with respect to the accuracy or completeness of the contents of this book and specifically disclaim any implied warranties of merchantability or fitness for a particular purpose. No warranty may be created or extended by sales representatives or written sales materials. The advice and strategies contained herein may not be suitable for your situation. You should consult with a professional when appropriate. Neither the publisher nor the author shall be liable for any loss of profit or any other commercial damages, including but not limited to special, incidental, consequential, personal, or other damages.

For international translation, contact the author at madanbirla@gmail.com

Book Cover Photo taken from iStock with permission.

Illustrations by [Illustrator]

First edition 2024

ISBN:

To:

Shayli, Shaan, Kayan, & Rohin

who have been a constant source of fun and

make my life journey a very enjoyable one.

Contents

I

A Book for and by Technical Leaders

"Madan, I could personally relate to the leadership challenges with technical support folks in particular, who I promoted to management because, like FedEx, we promoted from within. Many of my managers were great with the products, tech skills, and technology but were ill-equipped to handle the 'people' part of their job. I also really like the statement that you point out and recognize that the 'lack of awareness that leadership is a completely distinct skill set – more of an affair of the heart (right brain) than the head (left brain).' Also, the quote, 'But to lead, being smart isn't sufficient. You have to connect with people so that they want to help you move the organization forward' That hit home with me, and I believe it is very true!"

— **Jay Myers**, CEO, Interactive Services Inc.

The low leadership scores on my first employee survey and the follow-up one-on-one meeting requested by my boss made me realize that I have been relying on my highly developed analytical and technical skills – my left brain.

CHAPTER 1

Why Write This Book?

After completing my graduate studies in Engineering at the Illinois Institute of Technology in Chicago, I joined RCA in Indianapolis as an Industrial Engineer. I received promotions every couple of years, from Engineer to Senior Engineer to Project Engineer to Manager of Warehouse Distribution Systems. I was happy and not actively looking to change jobs when a headhunter approached me with an opportunity at the FedEx headquarters in Memphis. The combination of the challenge provided by a new and growing business and living in a warmer climate motivated me to make a move to join FedEx as Manager of Materials and Resource Planning.

At FedEx, all employees participate in a detailed annual survey on the company's culture and their leaders' performance. It's a vital measurement of the company's PSP — People, Service, Profit philosophy. Following my first survey, I was asked to meet Mike, the senior vice president of my division. Mike said, "Madan, you know we brought you from RCA to help take FedEx's Materials Planning department to the next level to support our double-digit growth and international expansion, but what I'm hearing from your staff is that they are not with you and your survey's leadership index score reflects that. You have excellent technical skills and need to improve your people leadership skills. I know you can do that. Let me know how I can help you."

I left Mike's office confused, thinking, "What did he mean, saying my team is not with me? Our service and inventory levels (the two key performance indicators in Materials Planning) are trending in the right direction. I'm a good manager. We are developing and implementing new inventory planning models and systems on schedule. Yet, if the division's senior vice president, my boss's boss, took the time to voice a concern, for my career's sake, I must address it."

My preferred method for learning new skills has always been taking college classes and reading books. In Indianapolis, while at RCA, I had already begun adding business knowledge to my engineering background. I was enrolled in Butler University's MBA program and started taking Finance, Economics, and Accounting classes. Following my conversation with Mike, I needed to learn about human behavior and develop people leadership skills, so I started taking Psychology, Human Development, Sociology, and Counseling courses at the University of Memphis. Before I knew it, I had enough credits to earn a master's degree in counseling.

From all the leadership books I read and my college courses in psychology, I distilled the following learnings:

- There is a thing called **feelings**, and people's feelings are the most crucial factor influencing their behavior.
- Leadership influences people through day-to-day behaviors, so they feel inspired to give the gift of discretionary effort* – their commitment and ideas. Discretionary effort cannot be forced. Employees choose to give it only when a leader's day-to-day behavior makes them **feel.**

    - *Part of a winning team going somewhere.*

- *I'm making a difference.*

- *I'm respected and cared about as a whole person.*

- *I'm recognized when I go above and beyond.*

- *I feel listened to when I have ideas to share*

- *I'm supported in my life beyond work.*

- *I'm challenged and growing professionally.*

In the leadership process for inspiring and engaging people, the key word is **feel**.

**Over the years, the founder & CEO of FedEx, Fred Smith, has frequently been asked this question: "What is the key to FedEx's phenomenal business growth and success?" His response has always been, "Our employees' discretionary effort."*

- Three distinct and equally important skill sets are needed in a manager to add maximum value: Technical, Managerial, and Leadership.

- Leadership is an altogether different skill set. It is more an affair of the heart (right brain) than the head (left brain).

"Supported by authority and regulations, you can get people to work at 60 to 65 percent capacity – just enough to satisfy minimum job requirements. Leadership is a multiplier factor that deals with the other 35 to 40 percent. A mere administrator can achieve average results. The leader gets superior results from average people. Management is largely an action-oriented cerebral process. Leadership is an action-oriented interpersonal process."

— **James J. Cribbin,**
Leadership Strategies for Organizational Effectiveness

Before this education and awareness, I had relied on my highly developed analytical and technical skills – my left brain. These skills made me an excellent engineer and effective manager but not a very inspiring people leader. With my new insights, I noticed that I was not alone in this predicament. Most of my contemporary professionals and managers in highly analytical fields like engineering, information technology, finance, and accounting were facing similar people leadership challenges.

I joined FedEx in its early days when the company was experiencing double-digit growth. To meet the day's demands and support future growth, all departments were expanding rapidly. The company had a strict policy to promote from within. Consequently, employees sorting packages moved up the corporate ladder, getting promoted to analysts, managers, and directors as their departments grew. A downside of this growth was that although loyal and committed, the middle management tier was riddled with insecurity. *You walk into a staff meeting and find the director intensely uncomfortable with anyone challenging his ideas. With him, it's "my way or the highway." He raises his voice, insults others, and micromanages his team, behaviors that are not conducive to driving employees' creativity and commitment. He has been through leadership training and is aware of desired leadership behaviors,* but with a high school education and lack of experience in the field, he feels insecure. **The less secure we feel internally, the greater our need to control things and people externally.** Insecurities make us want to appear more knowledgeable, accomplished, and confident before others.

"Madan, yes, as a former HR manager for two high-tech companies, I saw what you are saying in real time. The technical managers were not taught how to lead others during their college experience. Everything is either black or white. It works or won't work; there are no grey areas in their line of work. Kind of math, 1+1=2, and nothing else. That causes a real challenge to leaders

to create a synergistic team, inspire creativity, and welcome other approaches to solving problems."

— Robin Robinson

For sustained business growth in the 21st century, Leading for Innovation and Growth leadership is needed at all levels of an organization. Historically, leaders have looked for "the big idea," but now they must build a continuous capacity for innovation in their organizations. Starting a business with a killer product or service does not guarantee ongoing growth and market leadership.

Now more than ever, organizations' growth and profitability depend on the effectiveness of human performance. The greatest challenge in leadership development is learning how to unlock the unused potential in oneself and others. This book is designed to meet this urgent and global need of technology professionals, drivers, and leaders in today's knowledge economy.

There is enormous untapped potential in the employees of most large organizations. The ability to tap that creativity and latent commitment of everyone in the workforce is demonstrably the unifying thread in the achievements of all great organizations.

"We have also done a lot to leverage our technology and invest in capital improvements to enhance productivity and quality. We have added new plants, CAD/CAM, robotics, computers, and office automation. But the robot hasn't been invented yet that can take the place of a really creative manager or an enthusiastic and motivated worker."

— Donald Beall,
President and COO, Rockwell International

As part of my process for writing books, I send the drafts of completed chapters to selected people, representing the target audience, for their feedback.

One sample: "There's good, compelling content here. Your personal stories and examples make it interesting to read. The stories you have from other leaders and companies keep the content engaging. You may want to comment on why this book is different. As you put it, I found myself intellectually agreeing with the case for being a better leader, though then I found myself looking for the How. What tactically should I be doing to change?"

Based on this and similar feedback, I added the following two chapters, **'How is this book DIFFERENT from the other leadership books?' and 'HOW TO apply the leadership lessons from this and other books you have read.'**

CHAPTER 2

What makes this book different from other leadership books?

We, the technical/analytical professionals, are programmed and think differently.

Yes, the market is full of leadership books, and the technical professionals this book addresses have read these generic leadership books. But they do not help us because we, the technical/analytical professionals and managers, are programmed differently by our education and training. The sixteen years of schooling we undertake toward our bachelor's degrees have helped us develop our analytical left brain. For people completing graduate school, like me, there are another two years of still more analytical programming.

A book by and for the technology professionals.

This book shares proven and practical lessons, learned not just by me but also by other fellow travelers – technical professionals from different companies – on our successful journeys for understanding and applying leadership skills; lessons coming from analytical professionals and managers in technology, finance, engineering, accounting, and other fields the readers can relate to. It presents real-world ideas from leaders at Apple, FedEx, Google, Audi, Hilton, Microsoft, IBM, and others for making a successful transition from a technical professional to a business leader.

This book starts with where you are...

To help a person climb up to higher ground where you are standing, you have to reach down and extend your hand to the person where he is standing. That is, you have first to understand where they are at. How do they see the world? How do they comprehend the responsibilities and the skills required to be successful in their new roles? Once they feel understood, they are ready to listen to and see the big picture, visible from the higher elevation – the responsibilities and corresponding skills required to succeed in the new position.

I spent the last three years at FedEx at the Leadership Institute. The Institute's philosophy was that rather than using the HR people to do the leadership training, they selected people from the Operations to facilitate the leadership classes—people who had proven to be good leaders. The idea was that since you came up through the ranks, you can relate to the environment and responsibilities of the new managers. You got nominated by your division's senior officer for the facilitator position, and if selected, you received a bonus. It was a two-year assignment. After completing your term, the company guarantees you an equal or better position. The idea is that not only did you help the newly promoted managers in their growth, but you also grew as a leader as you got a chance to reflect on your leadership performance. "What was I doing right? What could I have done better?"

The Institute offered three week-long leadership development classes: LP1 – Leadership Practices 1 for newly promoted frontline managers, LP2 – Leadership Practices 2 for newly promoted Senior Managers, and LP3 - Leadership Practices 3 for freshly promoted managing directors. Within the first six months of getting promoted worldwide, the company required the person to attend these weeklong leadership development classes in Memphis, the corporate HQ.

On Friday, the last day of every class, the CEO, COO, or another senior management team member spoke to the class. In all the LP3 classes I co-facilitated, Fred Smith, founder and CEO, stopped by Friday morning and spent 45 to 60 minutes sharing his thoughts and answering participants' questions. He talked about the company's current performance, the growth strategy, and his expectations for their new role. The three expectations he shared in every class were:

1. Your leadership in leading your teams is the key to FedEx delivering its promise to customers, day in and day out.

2. You know your operations and part of the world better than anyone else in the company HQ. I'm counting on you to tell us if some aspects of our growth strategy do not make sense in your area.

3. The only thing we don't challenge at FedEx is how we treat people under our PSP (People, Service, Profit) philosophy. Everything else in operations must be continually challenged with creative and innovative thinking. What can we do differently to serve our customers better?

I led the team, responsible for updating the material and facilitating the LP3 class. After facilitating our first LP3 class, Mike, my co-facilitator, and I observed that the directors needed to be more fully engaged and interested in learning new skills. Their thinking and attitude were:

"I know what got me this promotion, so I'll keep doing what got me here. I'm in this class because FedEx required me to be here. I did a great job as a manager. That's why I got this promotion. I'm good and don't really need to learn new skills."

To address this problem, Mike and I worked with Thonda, the course designer, and developed a new two-hour module to start the class. This module addressed the following five gaps between their understanding and the reality of their new position and responsibilities.

1. Lack of understanding that leadership is an entirely different skill set from technical and managerial skills

After introductions, we started every new class by asking participants, "What is different about your new position compared to the one you had before?" Operations directors would say they now managed a more extensive geographical area; Support function directors would say they now had more staff under them; and so on.

Then we would ask, "How about the increase in compensation? Do you know that half of your total compensation is variable compensation?" The variable compensation is made up of three different programs. You are familiar with the MBO (Management by Objectives) program. The other two are LTI (Long Term Incentive) and Stock Options grants. The payout on all of these programs is based on business profitability. Maximizing your compensation and adding full value in your new position will require expanding your orientation from functional to business and tactical to strategic.

We would then present a slide (*Figure 2.1*) on the screen and ask, "What does this figure tell you?

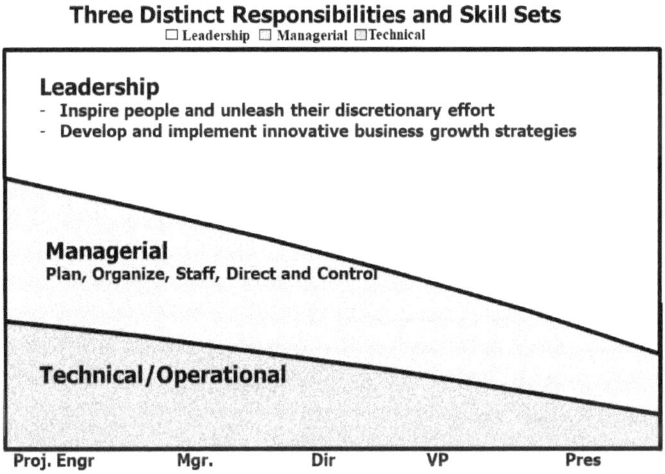

Three Distinct Responsibilities and Skill Sets
☐ Leadership ☐ Managerial ☐Technical

Figure 2.1

To add value as directors, we need to fulfill three responsibilities – Technical, Managerial, and Leadership – for which we need three distinct skill sets.

I have lost count of how many directors caught me during the break to say, "I had no idea that leadership and management are different skill sets." Chapter four goes into more detail on each responsibility and the corresponding skillset.

2. Lack of understanding that people leadership is more an affair of the heart than the head

Being an effective leader means influencing and encouraging employees to give more than just the minimum daily requirement. It brings out their creativity and commitment. Employees choose to give the gift of commitment when their leaders' day-to-day behavior makes them feel appreciated, listened to, and recognized. *Feel* is the keyword here. Innovation does not just happen mechanically. It must be actively supported and nurtured. The creativity of individual employees is the source of Innovation. Leaders must create an environment where employees feel comfortable suggesting and experimenting with new ways of doing things. Chapter six will address this and the unfortunate lack of insight into human behavior.

3. Lack of understanding that time and energy spent in building relationships adds far greater value than staying occupied with solving technical problems

There will be trouble when leaders do not carefully balance their time between technical, managerial, and leadership tasks. Leadership tasks commonly end up being prioritized lower than technical and managerial tasks. A leader's "inbox" never gets cleared, so they never seem to have time to talk to employees one-on-one. Leadership behavior – the benefits of which are realized over a medium to long term – does not give the instant payoff or immediate sense of accomplishment one gets from solving a complex technical problem. Naturally, anyone seeking an instant reward will take the shortest path and gravitate towards spending more time 'managing things' than building relationships. Chapter seven offers practical ideas to address this issue.

4. Lack of interest in and knowledge of what is happening in the larger business environment

Too often, leaders are focused internally – fully occupied with what is happening inside their organization. There is no process or expectation to keep up with the changes in the larger business environment they compete in, i.e., the external world. Louis Gerstner, the newly appointed CEO of IBM, noted in 1993, "IBM failed to keep pace with significant change in the industry. We have been too bureaucratic and too preoccupied with our view of the world. We have been way too slow getting new things to the market." Chapter ten will discuss in detail the critical role of 'Looking Out the Window' in developing strategic thinking and planning skills.

5. Lack of understanding that Innovation is a people process and a team sport

In her landmark book, *The Change Masters,* Rosabeth Moss Kanter described a three-step innovation process: "Innovation is the generation, acceptance, and implementation of new ideas, processes, products, or services. It can thus occur in any part of a corporation, and it can involve creative use as well as original invention. Application and implementation are essential to this definition; it involves the capacity to change or adapt."

People first generate creative ideas. At its inception, the fresh idea is raw. It must still be fully developed and may impact multiple operational or functional areas. People from these affected areas must accept and help fully develop a creative idea for implementation. Finally, it is people once again who implement the fully formed idea. The process involves an increasing number of people as it progresses through the three stages. Chapters eight and nine present practical and proven ideas for successfully engaging people in the innovation process.

Finally, the book addresses the vital reality ignored by other leadership books. They treat professional life as something separate from a person's personal life.

Leadership is an extension of you, the total you — your knowledge, skills, belief systems, life experiences, feelings, and education.

As discussed in the first chapter, after I met with Mike, I started taking classes to understand human behavior, mine and others. For one of my grad school psychology courses, I wrote a term paper titled "Leadership Excellence and Balanced Life." The theme of the paper was that leadership is an extension of you, the analytical you, the feeling you, the human you with human needs. Anything in your personal life that impacts you positively or negatively also impacts your performance on the job, especially your people leadership. I sent a copy of the paper to Fred Smith, founder and CEO of FedEx. A week later I got a call from his secretary who said that Fred would like to meet with me.

Fred started the meeting by saying, "Madan, I read your paper and agree with what you are saying." He waved a hand toward the offices of other senior officers on the floor and continued, "If they want to work sixteen hours, what can you and I do?" My response was, "When I arrive at the office at 8 a.m., I can't flip a switch in my head and say, 'Okay, I'm at work now, so I'll forget about everything else going on in my personal life.' If I argued with my wife last night, it comes to work with me. I'll give the minimum daily effort required so I don't get fired. Still, for the kind of company you are trying to build, you need all your managers to be fully operational if we are to take FedEx to the next level of growth and excellence. You are paying us for our creativity and the quality of our decisions, for getting the best out of everyone on our teams. You're not paying us for the hours. As I said in my paper, unmet life needs do not disappear. They create internal conflict and stress. A stressed mind is not in creative mode; a stressed mind is in survival mode. It is in FedEx's interest that leaders enjoy a balanced life and meet all their life needs, so when they come to work, they are fully here."

Fred asked me to work with Roy, the head of FedEx's Leadership Institute and develop a course on this subject for the company's leaders. I facilitated a two-day "Leadership Excellence and Balanced Life: A Nurturing Relationship" class for several years for FedEx executives.

"A stable, mature, and happy family life allows one more time and energy to devote to the workplace than a family life fraught with problems. Putting it differently, avoiding a bad family life may pay off."

A study by Cappelli of Wharton School, Jill Constantine of Williams College, and Clint Chadwick of Wharton contradicts other studies and the conventional wisdom that those who put family over career will earn lower wages.

The author is uniquely qualified to write this book

The ideal combination of firsthand experience in progressing from a technical professional to a successful business leader, counseling psychology and human behavior knowledge, and application of that knowledge in executive coaching, consulting, and leadership training.

– Education: B.S. in Mechanical Engineering, M.S. in Industrial Engineering, MBA (Finance), M.S. in Counseling Psychology

– Extensive Corporate Experience: From Engineer to Managing Director, leading a team of 100+ technical professionals, IT, Engineers, and Trainers

"Madan, thank you for sending this. I could not read it all, but selected readings herein convinced me that you are very perceptive of the human race's foibles and aspirations. Best, Fred"

A handwritten note from **Fred Smith, FedEx CEO,** on my manuscript "Leadership Excellence and Balanced Life."

– Consulting and speaking at global companies such as Google, Microsoft, IBM, Infosys, Tata Consulting Services, Bridgestone, SONY, Marriott, Hilton, and many others

– Facilitating "From Technology Professional to Innovation Leader" and "Leadership Excellence and Balanced Life" workshops at technology companies and graduate business and engineering schools

It does not just list the desired leadership practices but helps the readers make them part of their day-to-day behaviors.

One frequent feedback I hear in my Work-Life Balance workshops is, "We know what's the right thing to do, so why don't we do it?" Simple example: to enjoy good health, we all know we must eat right, exercise regularly, sleep for seven to eight hours, minimize stress, and build and enjoy healthy relationships. Knowledge alone is not sufficient to change behavior and make different choices. Internal and external factors come into play, some unique to an individual. It helps them understand the thought processes, beliefs, feelings, and other factors that drive their choices, priorities, actions, and reactions. The next chapter focuses on bridging the gap between knowledge and applying leadership lessons.

CHAPTER 3

HOW TO apply the lessons from this and other leadership books you have read

Knowledge about anything does not automatically lead to application and the desired behavior. Bridging the gap between knowledge and application is a process and requires conscious effort. The four steps in this process are:

1. Knowing. Yes, knowledge about the leadership role as you move up the corporate ladder is the first and essential step. Internalized knowledge about leadership responsibilities and practicing the corresponding behaviors are the keys to success in the new role.

2. Wanting. Developing people's leadership skills requires learning new behaviors and changing some old behaviors. Changing human behavior is challenging and requires persistent effort. A psychiatrist friend used to tell the following joke at dinner parties: "How many psychiatrists does it take to change a light bulb? One. But the bulb **must want** to be changed." The solid inner desire motivates the following two steps. The manager must have a personal motive for **why** they want to learn and apply the new leadership skills. The German philosopher Nietzsche's famous quote describes this step well, "He who has a 'why' to live for can bear almost any 'how.'"

3. Doing.

"What we have to learn to do, we learn by doing."

Aristotle

How did we learn anything in life? **By doing it.** To learn how to drive, after gaining knowledge from reading the driver's manual and securing our learner's permit, we had to get behind the wheel and go. I learned by driving in the parking lot and moving to side streets before getting on a busy highway.

4. Practicing and continually reminding the 'Why'. How do we get good at anything? By practicing it. After playing tennis for many years, a few years ago, I started playing golf. To get started, I took several lessons from a golf pro. The pro emphasized that regular practice is the only way to make the new swing consistent throughout the golf round. My goal to improve my handicap motivates me to hit practice balls at a driving range regularly. Similarly, practicing the new behavior is the key to making the new leadership skills part of your natural leadership style, your people personality.

Let us take a detailed look at each of the four steps.

New roles require new skills. Moving into the manager role requires three distinct skill sets: technical, managerial, and people leadership. A leader's people leadership skills are their day-to-day behavior and how they work with and relate to people.

After moving into the management position, our role becomes more value-added. We add value in areas that we spend our time on. In addition to learning new skills, it requires **a change** in choice-making behavior for where to spend our limited time and energy.

As discussed in the second chapter, the "I already know' thinking on the part of the newly promoted managers gets in the way of learning the leadership skills required to succeed in the new role.

"The other big obstacle to the willingness to learn is the urge to present yourself as always already informed. The philosopher Jonathan Lear calls this attitude knowingness. He regards it as a sickness that stands in the way of gaining genuine knowledge. It is "as though there is too much anxiety involved in simply asking a question and waiting for the world to answer," he writes."

— Jonathan Malesic,
The New York Times, January 3, 2023

As discussed earlier, any growth process starts with a reflective conversation with the self. Here are some questions to get you started.

1. What's my goal in this new role/position?

    As in my previous roles, I also want to be a big success in my new role, too.

2. In this new role, what are the key drivers of my success?

    The people on my team, as my performance is cumulative of everyone's performance.

3. What are the responsibilities and the corresponding skill sets?

    I must do my part in helping everyone on my team do their best.

The three areas of responsibility are Technical/Operational, Managerial, and Leadership. Leadership is different from management.

4. Evaluating myself against the three skillsets, what am I good at, and where are the gaps (self-awareness)?

5. What is my plan to bridge the skill gap and be successful in my new role?

It's an ongoing process because as we climb up the corporate ladder and assume more roles on and off the job, the demands exceed our available time. Occasionally, we must have this conversation to remind ourselves of the big picture and the goal.

A successful transition and lasting change require work in the following two related and mutually supporting areas:

1. THINK. Developing a new mental model reflecting the unique role

2. DO. Putting leadership behavior in action

In the Work/Life Balance workshops, I discuss reclaiming your life one day at a time by making the calendar work for you.

Your calendar represents your life, not just your work obligations, appointments, meetings, and commitments to others. The previous chapter discussed that once we move into management, we must balance our time between the three responsibilities: technical, managerial, and leadership.

Do: Along with scheduling work/business activities, schedule personal/family, exercise/leisure activities on the weekly calendar and your work-life balance priorities. In your work activities, make sure the calendar reflects a balance between leadership, technical and managerial responsibility, and corresponding actions.

Making a change is an inside-out process. It starts with THINK, changing the script/belief system to reflect the new role. As discussed earlier, the most critical element in successful change is WHY? The internal motivation: Why must I make this change? Because I want to grow and be the best leader I can be. Because I want to be successful in my new role, I want to add the maximum value. I need help to achieve the department's goals. The motivation can come internally, a desire for growth, or externally, when the pain of not changing (external consequences) is more than the pain of changing. The next chapter explores the whys for learning and developing specific leadership behaviors. The why keeps us on track when we begin to slip back into old habits.

The experience reinforces what we know. Over time, with persistent effort, the behavior becomes internalized – a new habit – and we don't even have to think about it.

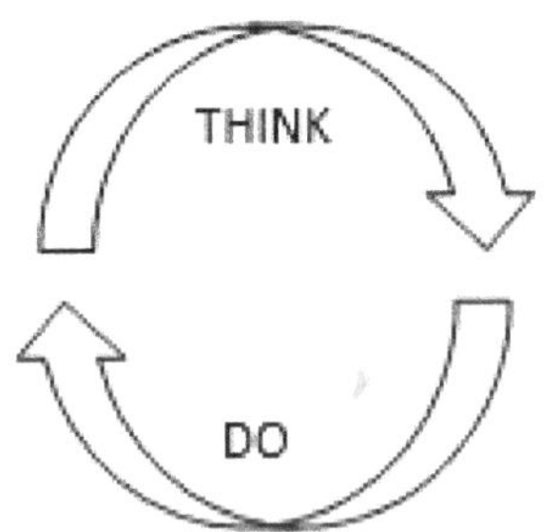

Figure 3.1

Another example of a new role script is the mental shift from task orientation to people orientation. Yes, tasks and projects have to be completed and delivered on time. But how you go about it changes. The focus becomes mentoring people for growth and trusting them to complete the tasks.

At the FedEx Leadership Institute, we used Team Trek's facility in Arkansas for our outdoor leadership and team-building classes.

I'm on Team Trek's mailing list. In the recent newsletter, Mike Gore, Chief Strategy Officer and Master Coach, shared a personal example from his first job.

"I'll never forget one conversation in particular. One day, I stormed into his office to vent my frustration about another department blocking our marketing plans. This was my first real job out of college, and I worked for Thomas. In the spirit of full transparency, I was a hothead back then. I was twenty-five years old, thought I knew everything, and had a short fuse with anyone who got in my way.

Thomas mostly listened as I relayed what had happened. I have no idea how long my rant lasted, but I eventually concluded and looked at him for an answer.

He said, 'Mike, you seem upset.' That was a gross understatement and not the response I expected. I was so obviously upset that anyone within earshot knew it. I'm sure I must have had a confused look on my face.

Reflecting on this moment, I can see that he was not asking if I was upset. The truth was he was more aware of my emotional state than I was. Rather, it was his way of calling attention to it. He was asking me to pause and see for myself how upset I was.

His shared observation had the intended outcome. I sheepishly acknowledged the obvious, now somewhat embarrassed by my emotional overreaction. I had half expected him to be just as upset as I was. After all, they were *his* plans that were being interrupted! His calm demeanor was disarming, to say the least.

And then he asked me a simple but life-altering question. 'Mike, how's that working out for you?' He was now grinning ear-to-ear because he already knew the answer.

Of course, it wasn't working out for me. That was his point, but he wanted me to arrive at the answer on my own. It was a profoundly convicting question that forced me to think about the natural consequences of my temper. That was the moment I saw my temper for what it was. Just as importantly, I gained clarity about how my lack of emotional self-control was hurting my influence and getting in the way of my goals.

When we ask people to think for themselves, we engage their hearts and minds. In effect, we are saying, 'I trust that you have the answer.' It is a powerful way to lead and one of the keys to influencing others. You see, Thomas didn't just tell me how to fix the situation that triggered my reaction. That would have been easy, but the moment would have been missed."

Following is an example of an engineering manager still operating under task orientation:

Bill, an engineering manager, hired Kathy, an engineering graduate from one of the top colleges in the country. After a few months, he assigned Kathy a critical project with a two-week deadline. Kathy was excited to get the project and worked hard on it. She submitted the report draft two days before the due date for Bill's review and feedback.

The following morning, she came in early, all excited to hear what the boss thought of her work. Just before heading out for lunch, Bill called Kathy into his office and said, "I read the report last night and found several errors. I corrected those, and here is your copy of the final report. It has already been delivered to my boss." Kathy felt very deflated.

I did not say anything to Bill after he shared this story with me. I observed that Bill's behavior was entirely driven by task orientation – "It's easier and faster to do it myself than taking the time to explain it to Kathy." The focus was short-term, immediate benefits versus making investments for better future returns. There was a lack of self-awareness in his role as a manager/leader; one of his responsibilities was helping people on his team grow and develop and be the best they could be.

"I know that the single biggest contribution I will make to this company is helping the next generation of leaders become the best they can be."

— A. G. Lafley,
CEO of Procter & Gamble

Let us look at how a little investment of time on the manager's part would have built Kathy's confidence and communicated that the boss cares about her growth and gains her trust and loyalty.

"You know, I must say this report is absolute proof that you worked extremely hard. It shows incredible detail and shows me that you put a lot of time and effort into it. But I'm wondering if we looked at this or recalculated this …"

With the latter approach, Bill could share his knowledge and experience, let Kathy make revisions, and produce the final report. Bill operated in a task-oriented mode and did not balance task and people/relationship orientation modes.

The African proverb "If you want to go **fast,** go **alone.** If you want to go **far,** go **together"** applies to leadership at work. Building a high-performance team and achieving big goals requires long-distance leadership.

Changing behavior is challenging. Developing people skills requires becoming a student of human behavior by asking questions such as: Why do I behave the way I do? What drives my behavior? Multiple factors influence our choices and behavior. Following is a partial list of these factors. We will explore these and other behavior drivers in detail in other chapters.

1. What we know. Knowledge, skills, our scripts for the various life roles

2. How we feel

3. Reinforcement from our environment, the positive or negative rewards from the environment.

4. Human tendency to stay in one's comfort zone

5. We spend our time on things we like to do and do them the way we know how

6. Cognitive bias toward activities that produce immediate/short-term results

7. The human/psychological need for maximizing pleasure and minimizing pain

8. The need for change that is understood intellectually but uncomfortable emotionally

9. What comes to us naturally; we think everyone else should be able to do it, too

10. We are creatures of habit, and the habits are hard to break

The final exercise in my Work/Life Balance workshops is for participants to develop a weekly personal Balanced Life action plan. At the top of the action plan page, I use the following quote by Annie Dillard: "How we spend our days is, of course, how we spend our lives."

How we spend our time determines the quality of our lives. Extending this thinking to work life, "As a leader, how we spend our days at work determines the quality of our leadership."

No manager walks into the office in the morning and thinks, "Today, I'm going to be an ineffective leader." The manager works long hours doing what he thinks is correct and in a way he knows. There is a considerable change in role and responsibilities once one moves from an individual contributor to a manager role, from a manager to a director role, and so on. The most significant change is that instead of doing the job himself, he gets the job done through people. That requires a different allocation of time and energy.

To help remind me of my goal of enjoying a balanced life, the photos of my children in my office were from when they were five or six years old. I kept the pictures the same as they got older.

The photos reminded me that they were growing up fast, and before I knew it, they would be leaving home for college. So every Monday morning, when I sat down with Carol, my secretary, to review the weekly calendar, we ensured that along with all the meetings, we included children's soccer/tennis/ballet/talent show. We also confirmed that I was not engaged full-time in a "management by meeting" mode and that there was some free time to think and walk around to talk to people in the department.

Yes, just as you become a successful technical and analytical professional, you have the capability and capacity to be a successful leader, too. You have proven that by using your passion and desire for growth, you became a qualified engineer, lawyer, accountant, systems analyst, and business analyst. The same attributes will help you become a good leader as well. The process is the same and requires developing and unleashing a different part of our brain, the right brain. People leadership is more of an affair of the heart (right brain) than the head (left brain). Let us get started.

NOTE

You will notice I repeat specific insights and practices in the book. The reason is that to change old habits and develop new ones, we need to remind ourselves.

II

21st Century's Leadership Needs

"You don't need to change – your survival is not mandatory."

— Edwards Deming

In today's fast changing business environment, the only way any organization can survive and thrive is if its internal rate of change exceeds the external rate of change. Is the external rate of change going to slow down? Absolutely not.

"The most important 'speed' issue is often not technical but cultural. It's convincing everyone that the company's survival depends on everyone moving as fast as possible."

— Bill Gates in his book,

'Business @The Speed of Thought'

Innovation is a team sport and a people process. Managers at every level of the organization need leadership skills to actively engage people in the innovation and the change processes.

"Apple's success depends on its culture and who it hires. For instance, the company typically seeks out employees with four shared skills: the ability to collaborate, creativity, curiosity, and expertise."

— Tim Cook,

Apple's CEO, at Univ. of Naples commencement ceremony

CHAPTER 4

The Type of Leadership Needed for Business Growth in the 21st Century

What keeps you awake at night?

Before accepting a speaking or consulting engagement with any organization, I request a 30-minute meeting with their top leader to tailor my remarks to the organization's needs. A key question I always ask is, "What keeps you awake at night?" The most common response – whether I'm talking to a CEO in San Francisco or Singapore, New York, Bangkok, Memphis, or Mumbai – is that "To continue to grow in today's fast-changing global economy, we must innovate and change. We cannot simply continue to do what we have been doing the way we have been doing it. We need to outthink and outperform the competition. We need innovation leadership at every level."

In one conversation, a CEO who previously worked in manufacturing and was now leading a large Technology Services organization shared, "In my previous job, we made money with machines. At night, when we went home, we could lock the doors, and when we opened the doors back in the morning, the machines were there. Now, we make money with people. How do we ensure that when we come in the morning, the people are all there, fully present and engaged in the enterprise? We make money by providing creative solutions to clients' business problems. How do we retain the best and the brightest and unleash their creativity?"

Creativity and innovation are keys to growth across all industries, as discussed by Daniel Lamarre, CEO of Cirque du Soleil, in his interview with Bloomberg Businessweek.

"During my 21 years at the company, we have expanded by leaps and bounds, with our touring shows reaching 450 cities in over 90 countries. Overall, more than 365 million spectators have seen our productions, and our 15 million tickets sold in 2019 were more than all Broadway shows combined. How did we achieve such astounding growth? I kept coming back to one word: creativity. One exciting innovation developed with Microsoft Corp. is a pair of augmented-reality smart glasses called HoloLens that allows our directors to visualize the entire stage before it's even built.

"Now that I've moved on from CEO to Executive Vice Chairman of the board, I plan to travel widely to spread my message: Whether you are an executive, an entrepreneur, or a professional, if you aren't placing a high premium on creativity, you're wasting your time. No company deserves to exist unless it's constantly discovering ways to make customers' lives better. Simply put, without creativity, there is no business."

— Daniel Lamarre
CEO, Cirque du Soleil

Why are they all saying the same thing?

Whether they are the CEO of a business enterprise or the president of a university, every leader is evaluated and compensated by their bosses (board of directors, trustees, etc.) based on one overarching question, "Over the last fiscal year, did you lead your organization to the next level of growth and excellence?" Leaders understand that no company exists in a vacuum. It exists in a larger business environment comprised of customers, competitors (local and global), government regulations, technology, and several other factors. If there is no change in the larger business environment, a company can continue doing business the way they have been and safely maintain its market share by growing in line with GDP. However, in a changing business environment, a company's internal rate of change (new business strategies, processes, products, distribution, etc., that the company can control) must match or exceed the external rate of change (outside the company's control).

If the external rate of change exceeds the internal rate, an organization will lose its competitive edge and market share. Companies like Kodak, RCA, Sears, Xerox, Blackberry, Borders, and many more that were once global market leaders in their industries lost a significant chunk of their market share along with their coveted leader status due to this very reason.

How did that happen?The arrows labeled E in Figure 4.1 represent the squeeze put on companies by the rate of change in the larger business environment (external changes) where competition occurs. The only way to neutralize this external pressure and gain market share is to counter it with a higher internal rate of change, represented by arrow I.

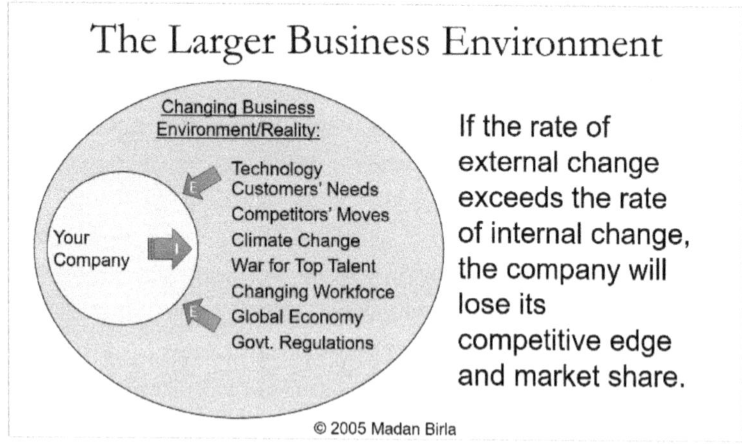

Figure 4.1

The first step in gaining market share is understanding the changes in the larger business environment. The second step is engaging the people in developing innovative solutions to capitalize on the opportunities presented by the changes. In today's fast-changing business environment, the speed in developing and implementing innovative solutions is the key to staying ahead of the competition and increasing market share.

Is the external rate of change going to slow down?

Absolutely not!

In fact, technological advancements have accelerated the rate of change. Consider how the evolution of one product – the iPhone – has impacted and transformed multiple industries like telecommunication, music, publishing, photography, gaming, e-commerce, and many more. When I started my career at RCA, the company manufactured Long Playing (LP) vinyl records. The rise of the Compact Disc (CD) reduced the demand for LPs, and streaming has all but eliminated CDs. RCA as a business does not even exist anymore.

Continuous innovation is the only sustainable competitive edge in today's fast-changing global economy. Netflix started as a video disc rental service, moved to streaming, and is now one of the world's biggest producers of movies and TV shows tailored for its international user base.

Who is responsible for change and innovation in the organization?

Everyone.

No matter how brilliant a CEO is, there are only 24 hours a day, and no single person can keep up with what is happening out there or have a monopoly over creative ideas. Leaders at all levels in an organization must look out the window and engage their teams in the innovation process, which involves generating, accepting, and implementing creative ideas. Good ideas are born when people with different perspectives work together on the same problem. Successful implementation of innovative ideas requires commitment at all levels.

'Leading for Innovation and Growth' requires two distinct skill sets.

1. People skills - to tap into people's discretionary effort, creativity, and commitment

2. Innovative Business thinking - to develop and implement innovative growth strategies informed by external changes

Microsoft's Leadership Principles and Practices

As discussed by Satya Nadella, Microsoft's CEO, in his book, 'Hit Refresh'

written with Greg Shaw and Jill Tracie Nichols, published in 2017 by HarperCollins, New York

(The bold highlights in the paragraphs are mine)

"Every organization will say it differently, but for me, there are three expectations – three leadership principles – for everyone leading others at Microsoft.

The first is to bring clarity to those you work with. This is one of the foundational things leaders do every day, every minute. In order to bring clarity, you've got to synthesize the complex. Leaders take internal and external noise and synthesize a message from it, recognizing the true signal within a lot of noise. I don't want to hear that someone is the smartest person in the room. I want to hear them take their intelligence and use it to **develop deep shared understanding** within teams and define a course of action.

Second, leaders generate energy, not only on their own teams but across the company. It's insufficient to focus exclusively on your own unit. Leaders need to **inspire optimism, creativity, shared commitment**, and growth through times, good and bad. They create an environment where everyone can do his or her best work. And they build organizations and teams that are stronger tomorrow than today.

Third, and finally, they find a way to deliver success, to make things happen. This means innovations that people love and are inspired to work on; finding balance between long-term success and short-term wins; and being boundary-less and globally minded in seeking solutions.

I love these three leadership principles. The heart of my message: **Changing the culture at Microsoft doesn't depend on me, or even the handful of top leaders I work most closely with. It depends on everyone in the company** – including our vast cadre of middle managers who must dedicate themselves to making everyone they work with better, every day."

When I was at FedEx, we had an initiative called 'Diplomat Visits' in which all managing directors were assigned a sales territory and were expected to make at least 2 sales calls during the year. The goal was to hear directly from customers about their business needs and experience with FedEx. This initiative aimed to develop business thinking and keep the business purpose front and center, which was 'creating and keeping customers.' More specifically, the goal was to ensure that the organization's people and processes are focused on meeting customers' needs and providing an outstanding customer experience because, for task-driven technical professionals, it is much easier to focus on departmental goals and internal performance indices.

On one of my diplomat visits, I accompanied a sales rep to a meeting with senior officers of a large international shipper. During the meeting, the customer shared that they signed a new pricing agreement last month but were still being billed at the old shipping rates. They were withholding payments until the revised invoices reflected the new lower rates. Due to nonpayment, FedEx's accounts receivable had put them on a cash-only basis. This situation was causing a lot of frustration for the customer and the sales rep. I promised to work on it upon my return to Memphis the following day.

After leaving the customer site, I asked the sales rep to educate me on the Memphis process responsible for this delay and lousy customer experience. He told me that five departments were involved in the process. A holdup in any one of them could delay new contracts taking effect – *Sales works with the Pricing department (under Marketing) during the latest rate negotiation phase; the negotiated price contract is then reviewed and approved by Finance and Legal; and following Finance and Legal approvals, Management Information System (MIS) department inputs the new rates into the billing system*. The process mainly worked, but occasionally, holdups led to unhappy customers, like the case I reviewed.

The first thing I did after returning to Memphis was to call up my peers in each of the involved departments and share the details of my diplomat visit. They committed to help resolve this situation as soon as possible. We organized a series of follow-up meetings to streamline the process and ensure this does not happen again. During these meetings, the root cause of this problem emerged clearly – the managers in each department were purely focused on their internal processes, as opposed to the holistic business process and customer experience.

There is a big gap between the CEO's 'need for innovation leadership' and the Technical Manager's performance on the job.

When working with organizations to develop 'Leading for Innovation and Growth' skills, I start the process by placing select employees and managers into four small groups and asking each group to answer one of the following questions:

Group 1: Why should you worry about innovation?

Group 2: What would innovation look like in your areas of responsibility?

Group 3: How do you create an environment that promotes innovative thinking at all levels of the organization?

Group 4: What stops you from developing and unleashing your creative potential?

The responses to the fourth question reveal, in most cases, that the leaders' behavior has prevented employees from engaging in innovative thinking and creative problem-solving.

Innovation-squashing leadership practices and organizational support systems typically include:

- Discouraging change

- Not open to looking at different ways to do things

- Micromanaging

- Resisting challenges by employees

- Bureaucratic systems that slow things down

- Indecisive management

- Busy schedules create a lack of time for creative thinking

- Turf protections and lack of collaboration resulting from departmental isolation

- Lack of challenging goals and direction

- Inability of managers to discuss conflicting ideas professionally

- Close-minded managers unwilling to entertain new ideas

- A culture that suggests one must not make waves and play safe instead

- Fear of failure

Most managers can articulate desirable leadership behaviors that will inspire employees and engage them in the innovation process. So why is there such a large gap between intellectual understanding of the right people's leadership practices and their application on the job?

Bridging this gap

The first step in bridging this gap is identifying its root causes, the five root causes discussed in Chapter 2.

1. Lack of understanding and internalizing' that leadership is an entirely different skill set from technical and managerial skills
2. Lack of understanding that people leadership is more an affair of the heart than the head
3. Lack of understanding that time and energy spent in building relationships adds far greater value than staying occupied with solving technical problems
4. Lack of interest in and knowledge of what is happening in the larger business environment

5. Lack of understanding that innovation is a people process and a team sport

Key points to keep in mind as you embark on this exciting professional growth journey

Leaders inspire people to do things above and beyond the ordinary. The processes involved in leadership are quite different. Leadership implies a higher function than management, although management is a critical element of effective leadership. You can 'manage' people to do what is already set out in existing processes, but it does not inspire them to give the gift of their creativity and commitment.

"The key change in leadership is from hardware to software. It's no longer command and control but connecting with people and getting everyone to pull towards the same goal."

— Barbara Kux
President, Nestle Polska Holding

Innovation is the generation, acceptance, and implementation of creative ideas. It is a people process and a team sport. It is a process that involves people in **mutually trusting relationships** freely sharing and building upon each other's knowledge to generate creative ideas. This is followed by people from all impacted areas **whole-heartedly accepting and developing** the raw creative ideas. Finally, the developed idea is successfully implemented by **committed people** across the organization unleashing their creativity to solve problems encountered during **implementation**.

Now more than ever, organizations' growth and profitability depend on the effectiveness of human performance. The greatest challenge in leadership development is learning how to unlock the unused potential in oneself and others. We – successful technical professionals – have the capacity to become 'Leading for Innovation and Growth' leaders.

I recently met with a Mumbai CEO who started a company, grew it into a market leader, and sold it to a German multinational. He said, "You know what keeps me awake at night? It's the first tee shot on the golf course in the morning. I have no idea where it's going to go." I can relate to this. While working at FedEx, I played tennis twice a week. After leaving FedEx, I had more time and switched to playing golf.

The next chapter focuses on how your strengths as technical professionals provide a solid foundation to build upon. Subsequent chapters will provide a road map for developing and unleashing your natural people leadership and creativity potential.

CHAPTER 5

Good News, Our Strengths Provide a Solid Foundation to Build Upon

The strengths that help us excel as technical professionals and managers provide a solid foundation to cultivate people leadership and innovative business thinking, i.e., the 'Leading for Innovation and Growth' leadership skills. These strengths are:

1. Systems thinking

2. Welcoming challenges and hard work

3. Analytical, logical, data-driven approach to problem solving

4. Technical expertise

5. Learning mindset and willingness to keep up with advancements in the field

6. Results orientation

7. Enjoying working with people

Learning and practicing new leadership behaviors is not a short-term project with quick results. Playing golf, I'm reminded weekly that knowing what to do does not automatically translate into doing it. I learned during lessons that you should keep your head down throughout the swing. One week, I had no problem keeping my head down, but the next week, out of eagerness to see where the ball was going, my head would rise early. We are creatures of habit, and changing habits is hard, so it demands commitment.

For any endeavor that demands long-term commitment and sustained enthusiasm, *why* is more important than *how*? Here's the 'why' that helped me learn and practice new people leadership behaviors – *"My performance is the cumulative performance of each individual I'm responsible for. Therefore, it is in my best interest to be the kind of leader that inspires and motivates everyone on the team to perform their best."*

I have closely seen numerous leadership development programs that badly miss their mark. They assume (incorrectly) that exposure to training and books is sufficient to produce growth; however, what is needed is a determination and growth mindset, which conveniently happens to be one of our existing strengths. I have seen motivated programmers pull out and read a 200-page user manual, cover to cover, to fix a pesky bug.

Becoming a 'people leader' requires a shift from left-brain to whole brain thinking, i.e., left + right brain thinking. The left half of figure 5.1 lists the left-brain attributes that help make us good technical, analytical professionals and managers.

Figure 5.1

The right-brain attributes make a manager a people person and a strategic thinker. The following is from Daniel Pink's book 'A Whole New Mind: Moving from the Information Age to the Conceptual Age.

"Our brains are divided into two hemispheres. The left hemisphere is sequential, logical, and analytical. The right hemisphere is nonlinear, intuitive, and holistic. These distinctions have often been caricatured. And, of course, we enlist both halves of our brains for even the simplest tasks. However, the well-established differences between the brain's two hemispheres yield a powerful metaphor for interpreting our present and guiding our future. Today, the defining skills of the previous era – the "left brain" capabilities that powered the Information Age – are necessary but no longer sufficient. And the capabilities we once disdained or thought frivolous – the "right-brain" qualities of inventiveness, empathy, joyfulness, and meaning – increasingly will determine who flourishes and who flounders. Professional success and personal fulfillment now require a whole new mind for individuals, families, and organizations."

The next chapter details why people's leadership is more an affair of the heart than the head.

We must step out of our comfort zones to grow as a leader and move up the corporate ladder.

Rob Carter is the CIO of FedEx and a key player in the company's phenomenal growth and global success. He is the recipient of numerous accolades, including *Fast Company's* Most Creative People in Business, *Fortune Magazine's* Executive Dream Team, three-time recipient of *Information Week's* Chief of the Year Award, seven-time recipient of *CIO* Magazine's 100 Award, and a charter inductee into the publication's CIO Hall of Fame. I asked him to walk me through his professional journey and point out the factors contributing to his growth and success.

"After receiving my Computer Science degree, I started my career as a programmer. After four years as an individual contributor, I was promoted to the manager of the group I was working in. I was good technically and produced results. At twenty-five, I was the youngest manager. I knew everyone in the group well. We were friends, went out bowling, and hung out after work. In the annual survey, my ratings as a leader were terrible. It hurt my feelings as I have never been rated so poorly.

"The division's vice president nominated me to move to another part of the company laterally. I interviewed for the position and turned it down. The VP called me and chewed me out. '*You are a coward and want to stay in your comfort zone. I overestimated you. Go, call back and say you made a mistake.*' I did, and they let me move into the new group. I was one of the fifteen managers on a big project.

"Since I did not know any of the people in my new group, I started there with a completely different mindset, as a leader instead of a friend. In going from being friends to being a leader, I

– Became far less selfish, not trying to appear cool but caring more about them and their projects

– Looked to lead by sharing the big picture

– Made expectations clear and held people accountable

"I was promoted to director of this large group of 15 managers responsible for a big, mission-critical project. I was identified by the company and asked to attend a weeklong leadership training class for high-potential directors.

"Things were going well professionally and personally. I got married, had a son, and completed the coursework for my MBA. The graduate courses in business helped immensely towards a deeper understanding of the business side. It was very valuable in helping me become a well-rounded business leader by complementing my technology background.

"A headhunter from an executive search firm started calling me about a job. I did not return his calls. He left a message saying he would be in Dallas and would like to have dinner. During the dinner, he told me the name of the company – it was FedEx. They made me an offer, and I accepted. When the president of my company heard about my resignation, he called to tell me that I was making a mistake by moving to FedEx as I was about to be promoted to VP.

"I was ready for a new challenge, and the opportunity to learn and grow helped me decide to move. Once again, I had to leave my comfort zone to leave a good position with a good company."

I have shared more about Rob's leadership philosophy in other chapters. It is human nature to want to operate in one's comfort zone. As professionals, we enjoy technical problems. We are good at tackling them. After moving into management, if we continue to spend most of our time working on projects, we will not add value as a manager. Indeed, solving technical problems provides immediate satisfaction and a feeling of contribution. While leadership activities do not offer the same instant gratification, their contribution to any team's overall performance is far more significant.

"Don't be afraid to expand; step out of your comfort zone. That's where the joy and the adventure lie."

— Herbie Hancock,
An American jazz icon and
fifteen-time Grammy Award winner

Herbie Hancock's life experience and creative compositions support this quote. From my corporate experience, that's where the business growth and professional promotions lie.

Our strength can become our weakness.

I was fortunate early in my career to have mentors who took an interest in my growth as a leader. I had just moved into management – managing warehouse distribution systems at RCA Music Service. I was in a meeting once, presenting the design of a new computerized system for automating 'pick and pack' operations in the warehouse. During that meeting, Paul, the director of warehouse operations, voiced several potential operational concerns, all of which I answered.

My boss, Dale, asked me to see him the following morning. He said, "I have feedback on your performance in yesterday's meeting, Madan. I know you did not mean to, but everyone else who saw you answering Paul's concerns felt that you were disrespectful to him. Your tone sounded impatient and indicated that you were dismissive of Paul's concerns. You interrupted him multiple times before he could finish stating his concern and started to explain how the system design addresses it. I think your impatience was because Paul was on step 3, and you were on step 6. I know you've been working on this project for six months, so all the operational and design details are obvious in *your* mind. Paul was looking at all of this for the first time. You need to recognize this and slow down. Let others catch up with you."

In college, my psychology professor said, "It takes two to know one." In our mind, we always do the right thing and treat people well. Only the recipient of our behavior or a neutral observer can tell us how we come across. When reading the local morning paper, I always look at the 'Horoscope' column for amusement. The day I was writing this chapter, my horoscope (Pisces) read, 'It's *a gift to know your weakness. Then you can aim for improvement and strength-building efforts productively*.' My lesson was that instead of allowing my ego to make me mad at people giving me negative feedback, I should be thankful for the gift of their insight.

During my warehouse automation meeting, the analytical side of my mind was engaged in solving a technical problem, so I failed to see the person/human interacting with me. This analytical approach serves us well when we are writing code or studying a database on a computer but not when we are working and communicating with people. How we share information is as important as the information itself. We must engage both sides of our brain – the analytical and feeling sides. Computers do not have feelings, but people do.

As individual contributors, we primarily relied on our technical and analytical skills.

As technical professionals, whether working on a project by ourselves or as group members, we primarily rely on our technical skills to complete tasks. After managing FedEx's Materials and Resource Planning function for ten years, I was promoted to Managing Director of System Form Engineering. The System Form Engineering department was a group of 80 professionals that supported the Memphis' superhub and other package sorting hubs around the world in doing the following:

1. Hub Design: Where and what size do the sorting hubs and airport facilities need to be in three and five years to handle the projected business growth?

2. Control room IT systems for monitoring and managing Hub's operations.

3. Engineering standards for workforce planning and measuring productivity

4. Designing training courses for training people performing the various functions in the Hub

I knew and had worked with most of the directors in the Memphis hub, but I wanted to officially introduce myself in the new role, so I set up brief meetings with them. Being my department's main 'customers,' I wanted to gauge their satisfaction with the support we were providing and what we could do differently to serve them better. They shared that they were satisfied with the technical side of the support and made suggestions about the future hub design. When I asked what we could be doing differently to better serve them, several directors said, "Just don't send your people to the hub and everything will be fine." We talked some more, and it became clear to me that there was a need to improve my team's people skills and help them forge better relationships.

Discretionary Effort — the key to FedEx's global business success

Following the release of my first book, *FedEx Delivers,* I was interviewed by Bloomberg TV in New York. The first question they asked was, "You joined FedEx in the early days and worked there for 22 years. Someone from planet Mars landed on earth and did not know anything about FedEx and asked you what has been the key to FedEx's business success? What would you tell him?" I answered, "That's easy. If you were to ask Fred Smith now or ten years ago, his answer would be, 'our employees' *discretionary effort.*'" Let me share a personal experience with you to explain what that means.

When I first joined FedEx, as part of my new employee orientation, I had to wear a courier uniform and ride all day with a courier in Dallas named Susan as she picked up and delivered packages. It was early 1980, and FedEx guaranteed overnight delivery by noon. That day Susan completed her deliveries by 11:15 a.m., and right after the last delivery, she checked in with other couriers in her part of town in case they needed help. Another courier named Bill radioed back and said he could use some help. Susan asked where his next stop was going to be, and we met him at a Walgreens location near that location. We transferred some packages from Bill's van to ours and delivered them promptly. Thanks to this last-minute collaboration, all packages were delivered on time that morning. I was amazed.

I asked if the other employees did the same thing she had done for Bill when they completed their deliveries. She looked at me with a bemused expression and replied, "Of course! Bill and other couriers have helped me out many times when I was struggling to make all my deliveries on time. We all know from experience that on a given day, some routes will be heavier than others. There may be traffic problems in a part of town or another issue. Everyone's goal in Dallas pickup and delivery operations is the same – on-time delivery to every customer daily."

This and many more similar experiences in my first few months at FedEx convinced me that there was something unique about the company's leadership that inspired employees to go above and beyond their duty and ensure the company's promise to its customers was kept.

My experience at RCA Records (my place of employment before joining FedEx) was that if an employee on a shift completed his production quota earlier than his shift schedule, he would sit in the break room until it was time to clock out; I was surprised at the unfamiliar practices of the FedEx employees.

As we move up the corporate ladder and assume greater responsibilities, the balance between the three skill sets shifts, and leadership becomes more important.

In his book, *Life and Death in the Executive Fast Lane*, Manfred Kets de Vries discusses that the derailment of a CEO is seldom caused by a lack of information about the latest techniques in marketing, finance, or production; rather, it is caused by a lack of interpersonal skills – a failure to get the best out of the people. If you continue to spend most of your time on technical and managerial tasks, fulfillment of your leadership responsibilities is bound to fall behind.

Karen Lynch, the newly promoted CEO of CVS, was in an interview with Bloomberg Businessweek discussing her professional journey. She shared, "At one point in my career, we had a huge issue in underwriting, and the CFO asked me to come in and run it. I said, *"I've got to learn underwriting."* He said, *"I don't need you to learn underwriting. I need you to be a leader."* I remember coming out of that job and the CFO saying to me, *"OK, what Finance job do you want now?"* I said, *"I want a P&L (profit and loss) job."* That was the start. It led to running bigger and bigger P&Ls, which got me ready for this job."

Leadership is different from management.

People often assume good managers are good leaders; however, management deals with the tactical operations of a job, while leadership involves inspiring and unleashing people's discretionary efforts. You manage systems and processes, but you lead people. Leadership requires balancing sensitivity towards people with the ability to get things done. You can manage but not lead without doing both.

Understanding the drivers of human behavior

As technical professionals, whether in IT or other fields, we all understand that to implement a successful change, we must first clearly understand the old system or product. Similarly, to successfully transition from individual contributor to inspiring leader, we must understand what drives our behavior.

These two reasons prompted me to take courses in psychology. The first was a skip-level conversation with my boss' boss shortly after starting at FedEx, in which he advised me to work on my people leadership skills. I wanted to understand the drivers behind human behavior in general and my behavior as a leader in particular. The second reason was to understand what influences our major life decisions. I had two young children when I joined FedEx, and maintaining a work-life balance was challenging. FedEx operated 24/7, and my department supported operations around the clock. I dig deeper into this in the 'Leadership Excellence and Work-Life Balance' chapter.

One of the courses I took was called 'Theory and Practice of Counseling and Psychotherapy.' This course covered various counseling theories in detail, including *Existential-Humanistic* by Frankl, May, and Maslow; *Client-Centered* by Rogers; *Gestalt* by Perls; *Cognitive/RET* by Ellis; psychoanalytic by Freud; and *Transactional Analysis* by Berne. In all my term papers and one-on-one conversations with professors, I focused on how these theories help elucidate human and leadership behavior.

Each theory has its view of human nature and a counseling approach based on that view. My distillation of the various ideas is that the most profound human need is to know and feel that '*I matter*.' How will I know if '*I matter*' to you in any relationship, whether professional or personal? When my needs, goals, and concerns are as vital to *you* as they are to me.

As an employee, my '*I matter*' needs are:

– Being part of a winning team that's going somewhere

– Making a difference

– Being challenged and growing professionally

– Being listened to when I have ideas to share

– Receiving recognition when I do a good job

– Being respected and appreciated

– Being treated as a 'whole person who has a life beyond work

When a leader meets these needs, their employees are actively engaged in the enterprise and willingly give the gift of their creativity and commitment, i.e., their discretionary effort. On the other hand, if these needs are not met, employees will gradually disengage.

Carl Rogers discovered that people make great strides in their personal lives when they feel genuinely listened to and understood. When managers employ the same principles at work, not only is the job done better, but they also build mutually trusting relationships.

Ellis' *A-B-C Theory of Personality* resonated with me by revealing why two people facing the same situation react differently. A (the Activating event) is the existence of a fact, an event, or the behavior or attitude of an individual. C (the emotional Consequence) is the individual's reaction. A does not cause C. It is B (Belief) that is the crucial factor in play. The Belief held by the individual about the Activating event leads to the Consequence or emotional reaction. In other words, the internal conversation – what a person says to themselves, their thoughts about the event, influenced by their belief system – determines their reaction. Rational beliefs lead to healthy behaviors, while irrational beliefs lead to unhealthy behaviors. This internal conversation may start consciously, but it becomes subconscious and automated over time. Thoughts and impulses travel fast on a familiar path along the neurons.

Our emotions and feelings directly result from our thoughts – what we say to ourselves – which are directed by our beliefs. In other words, our outer world reflects the blueprint of our belief system.

Beliefs ❯❯ Thoughts ❯❯ Feelings ❯❯ Behavior

Ellis' counseling process is based on the principle that changing unhealthy behavior requires examining and changing irrational beliefs and that people have the power to change their beliefs. The change process starts with D – <u>D</u>isputing irrational beliefs and replacing them with rational, healthier beliefs. The result will be E – new <u>E</u>ffect, healthy behavior, thanks to holding healthier beliefs.

I like to think of our beliefs working like a 'script.' As in a play, actors play their roles following the scripts given to them; we play our life roles guided by our scripts – our beliefs, formed by our life experiences, education, interactions with people around us, the environment we grew up in, etc. We have scripts for our roles and others in our lives and how they should behave. These scripts become a filter impacting how we view other people's actions and behaviors as good or bad.

Consider these examples of beliefs that drive behaviors at work: *My superior analytical and technical skills got me this promotion into management. My superior analytical and technical skills will be what I need to rely on for my future work success as well. Solving technical problems is where I make my most significant contribution at work.* These beliefs may have served us well in an individual contributor role but obstruct our path to being influential and inspiring leaders when we are responsible for leading a group of people.

"Most of us are slaves of the stories we unconsciously tell ourselves about our lives. Freedom begins the moment we

become conscious of the plot line we are living and, with this insight, recognize that we can step into another story altogether. Our experiences of life quite literally are defined by our assumptions. We make up stories about the world and to a great degree live out their plots. What our lives are like, then, depends on the scripts we consciously or, more likely, unconsciously have adopted."

— Carol Pearson, Ph. D.

The Hero Within: Six Archetypes we Live By

Going from here to there

Imagine visiting a state park and standing in front of one of their big maps to chart a path to the spot you want to reach. The first step to reaching your destination is to find your current location on the map. Similarly, in your professional journey from being a technical professional to becoming an inspiring leader, you must consciously know your current beliefs.

The following survey will help you do just that.

SURVEY:

The Journey from Successful Technical Professional to an Inspiring Leader

We – technical professionals – are by education and training, **programmed to think differently**. We favor left-brain (head) activities, **where our comfort zone lies**. We have the capability to develop and unleash our natural right-brain (heart) potential – our human side. It just requires adding new 'lines of code' to our existing program; our beliefs, scripts, assumptions, and view of the world, but first, we need to understand **our** current assumptions; our script; our program.

MAKE SURE YOU HAVE TIME TO REFLECT. There are no right or wrong answers.

	Rate each statement from 1 –5: **1** = **Does not** reflect my thinking **2** = **Somewhat** reflects my thinking **3....** **4 ....** **5** = **Accurately** reflects my thinking
As a technical manager I...	
1 ... tend to approach the world from a strictly rational perspective, i.e., through linear, logical thinking.	1 2 3 4 5
2 ... believe solving technical problems is where I make my greatest contribution at work.	1 2 3 4 5
3 ... get frustrated when people can't follow my logical recommendations or show resistance to my recommendations.	1 2 3 4 5
4 ... have a tendency to alienate people because I take a stand and am willing to fight until they 'see the light.'	1 2 3 4 5
5 ... believe everyone should be as self-motivated as I am and	1 2 3 4 5

employees should give me a reason to recognize them.	
6 … would rather just track down information myself because too often it takes employees too long to get me the requested information.	1 2 3 4 5
7 … believe that taking time to connect with people by listening to their career goals and personal concerns is desirable but it ends up falling behind other more urgent priorities.	1 2 3 4 5
8 … have found that things rarely get done correctly unless I do them or involve myself.	1 2 3 4 5
9 … interpret people's conversations literally; I tend not to look for hidden meanings in a conversation.	1 2 3 4 5
10 … find that when listening to a conversation, my tendency is to 'listen to	1 2 3 4 5

respond' versus 'listen to understand.'	
11 ... find that when an employee is telling me about a problem, my tendency is to immediately jump into problem-solving and start offering solutions before asking for that individual's inputs.	1 2 3 4 5
12...believe my superior analytical and technical skills got me this promotion into management.	1 2 3 4 5
13 ... derive satisfaction in proving others wrong and showing people my superior logical skills.	1 2 3 4 5
14...tend to bypass someone who has a history of showing resistance to my clear and logical recommendations.	1 2 3 4 5
15...believe that I should be able to outline to my employees what needs to be done and they should do it, giving their best (including discretionary effort, e.g., creativity,	1 2 3 4 5

commitment) without additional support and encouragement from me.	
16…believe my superior analytical and technical skills will be what I need to rely on for my future work successes as well.	1 2 3 4 5

Figure 5.2

Survey Scoring

The Journey from Successful Technical Professional to an Inspiring Leader

Record your rating for each statement from the survey in the **'Item Rating'** column below; then calculate the **'Average Rating'** for the two items that make up each category. An **'Average Rating'** of 3 or more may suggest that you expand your existing program by adding new 'lines of code' (insights and behaviors).

As a technical manager I:	Item Rating	Average Rating	Becoming a Successful Leader: Expand your existing program by adding these new 'lines of code'
1...tend to approach the world from a strictly rational perspective, that is, through linear, logical thinking. 9...interpret people's conversations literally; I tend not to look for hidden meanings in a conversation.	—— ——	——	The world is multi-dimensional. How people feel greatly influences how they behave and perform. People will not follow me unless they feel they can *trust* me. The key word is <u>feel</u>. I must learn to tune into the feelings behind other people's spoken words
5...believe everyone should be as self-motivated as I am, and they should give me a reason to recognize them. 15...believe that I should be able to outline to my employees what needs to be done and they should do it, giving their best (including	—— ——	——	People work for people, not companies. The quality of an employee's connection with their manager plays the most important role in motivation. **Being analytical all the time makes me inaccessible, so people feel shut out.** I need to allow others to see my human side. Relationship=Discretionary Effort

discretionary effort, e.g., creativity, commitment) without additional instruction from me.		61	
12...believe my superior analytical and technical skills got me this promotion into management. 16...believe my superior analytical and technical skills will be what I need to rely on for my future work successes as well.	———	———	My performance is cumulative of everyone in my department. My interpersonal/people/leadership skills determine the quality of effort from my staff, hence my success as a manager.
2...believe solving technical problems is where I make my greatest contribution at work. 7...believe that taking time to connect with people by listening to their career goals and personal concerns is desirable but ends	———	———	Developing and tapping 100% from everyone in the department is my most value-added contribution. To achieve this goal, I need to develop and apply all three skill sets: Technical, Managerial, and Leadership.

up falling behind other more urgent priorities.			
10...find that when listening to a conversation, my tendency is to 'listen to respond' versus 'listen to understand.' 11...find that when an employee is telling me about a problem, my tendency is to immediately offer solutions before asking for that individual's inputs.	—— —— ——		There are times when employees do not want me to solve their problems. They just want me to listen and understand.
13...derive satisfaction in proving others wrong and showing people my superior logical skills. 4...tend to alienate people because I take a stand and am willing to fight until they 'see the light.'	—— —— ——		Ask: "Is it a win for the relationship?" I need to keep in mind, "How does it feel to lose?" Frustration and resentment are not the emotions I want my peers and employees to feel after their interaction with me.

8...have found that things rarely get done correctly unless I do them myself. 6... I'd rather just track down information myself because too often it takes employees too long to get me the requested information.	—— ——	—— 	It feels great to help others to grow and succeed. When I am invested in their growth, they will walk over hot coals for me. I need to think and behave like a mentor.
3...get frustrated when people can't follow my logical recommendations or show resistance to my recommendations. 14...have a tendency to bypass someone who has a history of showing resistance to my clear and logical recommendations.	—— ——	——	Their resistance is not aimed at me. Resistance is a natural emotional reaction to change – fear of the unknown. I need to learn to tune in and help them express their feelings. Feelings pass and change when they get expressed directly.

Figure 5.3

After making just one small change, you will see immediate results in improved people skills. You do not have to make wholesale changes: just one step, **one belief at a time**.

III

Developing Your People Leadership Skills

"At one time, management rented employees' muscle: then, their brains. Now, however, it must win their hearts and souls in order to build teams committed to solving business problems on the run."

— Bernard Nagle and Perry Pascarella,
Leveraging People and Profit: The Hard Work of Soft

Management

Wanting employees to do their best requires an understanding of their basic motivational needs. People who are understood and treated as people come to work inspired. Employees who receive no praise or encouragement will do the minimum, so they do not get fired. They detach themselves from the environment and withhold emotional involvement. Feeling that one is seen – truly seen – and acknowledged by another person is one of the most joyous human experiences.

"In the Google context, we'd always believed that to be a manager, particularly on the engineering side, you need to be as deep or deeper a technical expert than the people who work for you. It turns out that that's absolutely the least important thing. It's important, but pales in comparison. Much more important is just making that connection and being accessible."

Adam Bryant of the New York Times wrote an article in 2011 titled *Google's Quest to Build Better Boss* which included the above quote from Laszlo Bock, Google's vice president for People Operations (Human Resources).

CHAPTER 6

People Leadership: More an Affair of the Heart than the Head

At the start of my weeklong leadership development classes at the FedEx Leadership Institute, I would ask the managing directors, "What is the one thing a leader must have before they can truly be a leader?" Their answers commonly include – business and operations knowledge, technical competence, management skills, communication skills, etc. In my view, these are beneficial qualities but not sufficient. Then, I would ask participants to visualize a situation, "I stand at a busy intersection holding a large sign over my head with my name and job title. The people driving by that read it may think I hold an important management position at FedEx, but if I turn around and find no one behind me, I'm not a leader." A leader must have followers – willing followers – to be a leader. John Boehner, retired congressman, and former House Speaker, said, "A leader with no followers is just a guy taking a walk."

Why would someone follow you? Employees will follow you if you meet their needs. The most profound human need is to feel that '*I matter.*' If I'm your employee, my needs should matter to you. To name just a few – the need to feel respected, the need to feel that I'm part of a winning team – a team that's going somewhere; the need to feel challenged intellectually and to grow professionally; the need to feel recognized when I do good work; the need to feel listened to when I have ideas to share…

Employees may admire your analytical and technical capabilities, but those alone cannot inspire them to follow you and willingly give the gift of their discretionary effort.

"We need to be listened to, taken in, and paid attention to. Very few people ever get any attention paid to them. So, the person who takes them in becomes thrilling to them. That's the way executives control (influence) people. And the leaders who genuinely have that quality are stars." (Harold Guskin, Hollywood acting coach)

Wanting employees to do their best requires understanding their basic motivational needs. People who are understood and treated as people come to work inspired. Employees who receive no praise or encouragement will do the minimum to avoid getting fired. They detach themselves from the environment and withhold emotional involvement. Feeling that one is genuinely seen and acknowledged by another person is one of the most joyous human experiences.

For Leaders as well as Followers

Feelings that boost performance & encourage discretionary effort	Feelings that block performance & discourage discretionary effort
Inspired Secure Trusted Appreciated Engaged Optimistic	Uninspired Insecure Distrusted Unappreciated Disengaged Pessimistic

Figure 6.1

The Performance Boosting Cycle

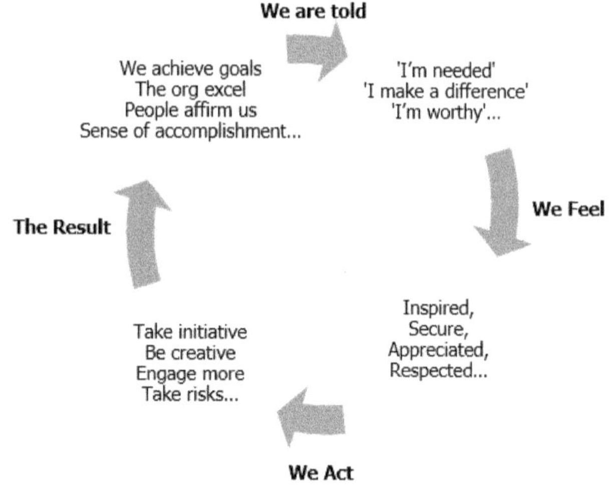

Figure 6.2

REINFORCEMENT FROM THE ENVIRONMENT: ROLE IN HUMAN BEHAVIOR

As I have shared earlier, my motivation to pursue graduate studies in counseling and psychology was to improve my people leadership skills. The starting point of this growth journey was to understand why people behave the way they do. What I learned is that human behavior is complex, and there's a multitude of factors that simultaneously influence a person's behavior. It would be presumptuous on my part to develop and present a model that tries to explain all human behavior. Instead, I'm sharing knowledge gained through reflections on my leadership behavior, close observations of my followers, peers, and superiors, and the theories I learned in psych courses. While there are many drivers, the following three play a crucial role.

– *What one knows and thinks:*

> This includes knowledge and skills (operational, technical, business, etc.) and one's personal belief system (our 'scripts') regarding on and off-the-job duties. I discussed On-the-job role scripts in chapter two. I will discuss Off-the-job role scripts in chapter eleven.

– *How one feels:*

> About oneself and others, perception of how others feel about them, on and off-the-job demands, and time pressures.

– *Reinforcement from the environment:*

> Both positive and negative, from people - staff, peers, bosses, customers, company policies, family, friends, and society at large. For instance, if a company's leadership repeatedly states that 'we must innovate and need creative ideas at every level of the organization,' but the people getting promoted are the ones that play safe and don't rock the boat or excel at office politics, the organization's

practices will have far more influence on employees' behavior than the management's pleas and sermons.

Let us look at some real-world examples of effective and ineffective leadership behaviors. We all have seen these behaviors in people we have worked with. The following discussion is adapted from John Powell's book *Why Am I Afraid to Tell You Who I Am?*

The Indecisive

If no decision is made, nothing can go wrong. With this orientation, the leader drags out the decision as long as possible, "Give me more information; do this analysis; and so on." By engaging in this behavior, the leader is protecting his fragile ego and self-esteem.

What One Knows/Thinks. He knows that as a leader, the buck stops at his desk. He is responsible for making the final decision after all possible options have been analyzed. He knows that this is frustrating his staff.

How One Feels. The manager fears losing respect if his decision turns out wrong. Why?

Reinforcement From the Environment. The manager has been criticized by his superiors for past mistakes.

In this scenario, the game's name is safety and self-protection, and the motto is – Nothing attempted, nothing lost. On the other hand, a person with a growth mindset learns from mistakes along their (successful) journey to becoming a more effective leader.

The Dominator

He can dominate people with his highly developed analytical skills and technical knowledge. This leader rarely, if ever, loses an argument. He does not listen well and appears to expect to learn little, if anything, from others.

What One Knows/Thinks. He is knowledgeable technically and very sharp analytically.

How One Feels. Because of a generally left-brain-driven analytical orientation in life and dealing with people, he cannot sense how his behavior makes others feel. The dominator is often bothered by subconscious feelings of inadequacy.

Reinforcement From the Environment. The manager has been recognized by superiors and the organization for his technical expertise. He has yet to be coached in 'people leadership' skills.

Fearful people can be very rigid. They put up strong defenses. Their cardinal rule is that they are always right.

The Cynic

The cynic is a demoralized un-realist. Things have failed to turn out how he wanted them, so he takes the pain of disillusion out on everyone.

What One Knows/Thinks. He can't trust anyone. The whole system is corrupt.

How One Feels. As long as the manager persists in his role as a cynic, he won't have to take an honest look at himself and his world nor go through the pains of adjustment to reality.

Reinforcement From the Environment. He lacks close relationships and is a lonely person behind his smirk. Most people ignore him. Sometimes, he successfully finds other cynics in the organization to reinforce one another.

The People Developer

This leader has a reputation for developing and promoting people. People want to work for him. He operates like a coach of a successful sports team – finds a raw talent and invests his time and energy in helping them develop and progress to the next level. As Harvey Firestone said, "*It is only as we develop others that we permanently succeed.*'

What One Knows/Thinks. He knows that his success and performance as a leader are cumulative for each person in his department. He knows that taking the time to share his knowledge and coach others is an investment he must make for returns further down the road.

How One Feels. He feels safe if someone in his department is more knowledgeable in certain areas. He actively looks for people who complement him. He feels good when people from his department get selected for more responsibilities.

Reinforcement From the Environment. His boss and the organization let him know that they look forward to interviewing and hiring people from his area.

The Delegator

This leader delegates not just tasks but also authority to make decisions. He is always available when an employee has a problem or needs to ask a question. He spends time sharing the big picture and building relationships across the organization.

What One Knows/Thinks. He knows he cannot do it alone and understands that the best way to develop people is to delegate responsibility and authority. Building relationships with his peers is a value-added role only he can play, and that helps his employees when they need information from other departments.

How One Feels. He feels secure in letting employees make presentations to senior management. He does not require them to clear everything with him before copying/responding to his bosses.

Reinforcement From the Environment. His employees like the exposure to senior management and go above and beyond for him. He enjoys a much healthier work-life balance than leaders who do not delegate.

The Competitor

The competitor must win in whatever he does. He makes everything a "win-lose" situation. He doesn't discuss; he debates.

What One Knows/Thinks. He thinks that being perceived as a loser is the worst thing for a person in a leadership position. He must win every time to prove his self-worth to himself and others.

How One Feels. He feels insecure and must consistently prove his worth through competition and rivalry. There are many causes of insecurity, such as lack of approval in his early life. His need for recognition intensifies the drive to 'get ahead.'

Reinforcement From the Environment. People can sense hostility towards anyone they feel is standing in their way or surpassing them. After a few interactions, people try to avoid or ignore him.

We all know leaders who are dominators, competitors, or cynics. The problems of leaders who attack subordinates, undermine their superiors, or have constant conflict with their peers are commonplace. Organizations pay an astronomical price for these behaviors.

ONLY OTHERS CAN TELL US HOW WE COME ACROSS AND MAKE THEM FEEL

During my tenure as managing director of materials and resource planning at FedEx, a reorg in another division resulted in two managers and all their staff being transferred to my group. As we walked out of the conference room after a long meeting, Darrell, one of the new managers, pulled me aside to say, "Madan, one of these days, when I win an argument over you, I will buy you a beer." From my drive home that evening until falling asleep, I kept thinking about what Darrell had said. I had no idea my managers were getting the impression that I had to win every argument. The environment I had unknowingly created around me was the opposite of what I wanted. I told them I needed their ideas and wanted them to feel free to voice them even if they went against my opinions.

I knew that for my staff to grow, they needed to handle projects and solve problems independently and in their way. Reflecting on my behavior revealed that one of the drivers of my negative leadership behavior was the inclination to involve myself in solving every problem and solve them my way. I rationalized it by thinking I was helping them by sharing my ideas and approach. Analytically and technically, it may have been valuable information, but this behavior made *them* feel, "*My ideas do not matter; I'm not as smart as Madan.*" It is not at all an example of effective leadership.

After this incident, I only offered my input to my subordinates when they asked. I was glad Darrell felt comfortable enough to share how I made him feel. From then on, I made it a point to actively seek feedback in my one-on-one meetings on what I was doing right and what I could do differently to help them become the managers they wanted to be.

One of the leadership gurus I greatly admire is Warren Bennis. His books were full of practical ideas; we used them at the FedEx Leadership Institute. The following message from one of his books helped me gain insight into my leadership behavior.

*If you're a leader, you've got to give up your omniscient and omnipotent fantasies – that you know and must do everything. Learn how to abandon your ego to the talent of others. There's a great example of this from 19th-century British history. Two dominant figures of that era were William Gladstone and Benjamin Disraeli. Gladstone was an influential public figure for more than 60 years. It was said that when you had dinner with Gladstone, you thought that **you were with** the most interesting, brilliant, and provocative conversationalist. And it was told that when you dined with Disraeli – an equally charismatic figure – you felt **you***

were *the most interesting, brilliant, and provocative conversationalist. If you're a boss, ask yourself which are you most like – Gladstone or Disraeli? There is a profound difference* [Warren Bennis].

For the June 1999 issue of Fast Company magazine, Pamela Kruger interviewed Dr. Paul Wieand, a successful bank CEO and founder of the Center for Advanced Emotional Intelligence (AEI), specializing in leadership development programs for top executives and entrepreneurs. AEI aims to "Turn ultra-achievers into 'learning leaders' – people with self-knowledge and emotional security to remain true to their 'authentic' selves and grow from criticism."

One of his clients, Jay Sidhu, CEO of Sovereign Bank, shared that he was taken aback when he learned how his staff viewed him. An avid reader of Tom Peters, Sidhu was determined to create "one of the best companies in America" and was committed to running a team-driven, inclusive organization. So why did his staff find him intimidating? "People who come to us always think they are a people person. They get a shock when they get results of their 360-degree evaluations," says Wieand. "I remember Jay asking me – 'Isn't *there one person who sees it the way I do?*"

THE POWER OF POSITIVE SPEAKING

We have all heard and read about the power of positive thinking. The best way to create a positive and receptive atmosphere for creative ideas is to utilize the power of *positive speaking*. Let's look at two versions of a common scenario.

Someone presents a creative idea.

Version A

You notice some problems and respond, "It won't work."

The presenter asks, "Why?"

You share your concern as to why you think it won't work.

The presenter answers with a possible solution to overcome the obstacle stated by you.

Instead of listening to the answer, your mind is thinking of the next obstacle you will bring up to prove that the idea won't work. As soon as your mind decided and heard it wouldn't work, its mission became to prove it.

Faced with the unending problems brought up by you, the presenter gets frustrated and gives up. Feeling "I wasn't listened to," the presenter vows not to voice their ideas to you in the future.

Version B

You respond, "That's a great idea and beautifully presented. Here's a couple of things I'm not clear on. Please help me understand..."

You share your concern as to why you think it won't work.

The presenter answers with a possible solution to overcome the obstacle stated by you.

This time, your mind is actively listening to understand the answer and not thinking up more obstacles. Your mind decided and heard that this is a great idea, so it wants to learn and understand more. Now, two minds are engaged in finding solutions to your genuine concerns.

Even though both minds could not devise a solution during the meeting, all of your concerns were addressed, and the presenter left the session feeling good. They feel "I was listened to and encouraged" and say, "Let me work on the unresolved issues, and I'll get back to you in two weeks."

The following statement presents an excellent way to brighten someone's day on and off the job. "Speak a true, loving word to someone. 'It makes me feel happy to see you.' 'I admire how you stay strong and positive through challenging times.'

'Congratulations on your recent success.' 'You inspire others around you.' Our words are powerful." (Carolyn Slok, *Science of Mind* magazine)

THE PLATINUM RULE

We all know the Golden Rule, "Treat people like you want to be treated." At the FedEx Leadership Institute, we discussed the Platinum Rule, "Treat people like **they** want to be treated." The underlying message is to find out what motivates each person on your team and use that knowledge in how you treat them. We are individuals with unique personalities and preferences. This rule is especially relevant now in the global workforce paradigm. Today, most technology teams have people from and in different countries. Every culture has some nuance in how they communicate and make decisions.

I teach a residential week-long leadership seminar for Executive MBA students at the University of Memphis. I have been using 'The Leadership Challenge by Kouzes and Posner as a textbook for this class, in which we discuss the following five leadership practices:

1. Inspire a Shared Vision
2. Challenge the Process
3. Enable Others to Act
4. Encourage the Heart
5. Model the Way

I cover one leadership practice daily and ask the students to submit a paper on it the following morning.

Homework Assignment Guidelines

Write an essay that:

1. Documents your understanding of each Practice of Exemplary Leadership.

2. Demonstrates your ability to link these concepts with personal experience.
3. Applies this analysis to your becoming a better leader.

Consider these questions:

a. What are the key ideas involved with this leadership practice? (Refer to the book chapters that address this.)

b. Reflecting on personal experience(s) describe what happened, and how does that situation (behaviors and actions) illustrate the principles involved in the leadership practice?

c. What was the outcome (feeling and impact) – especially if you were personally involved?

d. What did you learn from the experience, your reflection, and your analysis that you can apply now to become a better leader?

Be prepared to share your findings with others in the class.

The following is an excerpt from a paper by one of my students. The leadership practice is '*Encouraging the Heart*,' the quoted text addresses '*What did you learn*.'

"What I learned from the experience that will help me become a better leader is that I can get work done through others and add greater value to the organization if I can recognize what motivates each team member and give them what they want. A good leader's mutually trusting relationship with their employees is fostered by simply celebrating successes. Celebrating even small successes is just as important as celebrating the crossing of the finish line. Sometimes, the finish line is unclear in an organization that takes an agile approach to tackling problems and implementing solutions. So, taking the time to plot a milestone and measure progress to give a reason for celebration is very effective in nurturing the employees' hearts who, after all, are ultimately humans with feelings."

The following comment by Holiday Mathis in the December 19, 2022, edition of The Commercial Appeal presents the platinum rule interestingly.

"Relationships are like cooking. Some dishes work with few simple ingredients, and others require you to balance many elements, steps, and techniques."

THE BEST AND WORST LEADERS

James Cribbin, an author of 'Leadership Strategies for Organizational Effectiveness,' has asked managers at all levels to describe the characteristics of the most effective managers they have ever known. I have chosen just two of the many comments he shares in his book.

The Best Leaders

"She inspired confidence by having respect for and confidence in us. She often thought that I was better than I thought I was."

"He made us feel important and convinced us that our work was important."

The Worst Leaders

"She was demeaning. You rarely left her office without feeling worse about yourself and angry with her."

"He motivated through fear. As a result, he only got malicious obedience, the absolute minimum that had to be done."

The following quote, I heard somewhere, encapsulates the above experiences perfectly. "A good leader makes you feel good about himself/herself. A bad leader makes you feel bad about yourself. A great leader makes you feel good about yourself." (*Anonymous author*)

STEPPING OUT OF THE SANDBOX

Adam Bryant's column CORNER OFFICE in The New York Times featured his conversations with CEOs. The following is part of his interview with Deborah Dunsire, chief of Millennium: The Takeda Oncology Company, a biopharmaceutical company in Cambridge, Mass.

Q. *What leadership lessons did you learn when you first started managing others?*

A. I have typically worked hard and done well; sometimes, that desire translated into overdoing it on the leadership side. If something went wrong, I would get too anxious about it or think I had to fix it personally.

As I've stepped further and further outside my comfort zone, I've had to focus more on the work of leadership and not focus on being the person who solved the details of the problem. The focus on leadership means asking yourself, "What do I add?"

Q. *How did you learn that lesson?*

A. I heard gentle feedback: "You're in my sandbox, and we're not accomplishing a lot being in here together." I also heard feedback from a team I worked with: "Gee, we know you're good at this stuff, and you've done it, but sometimes we need to kind of bang our heads a little bit more without you fixing it."

So, I learned to step away sometimes and - in the right situation - allow a person to stub their toe. The work may not come in ideally, but the learning was much more effective, and people felt empowered to own the outcome differently.

"My most significant learning was the role switch from doing analysis to leading people." A conversation with **Reinhard Fisher, VP, Strategy and Chief Digital Officer Audi of America**

Reinhard joined BMW in Germany as an analyst and moved to the U.S. as BMW Network Development and Distribution manager. After three years, he joined Audi North America as Director of Sales Operations. As Vice President, he is responsible for Strategy, Digital Operations, and Training for Audi North America.

Madan: What leadership lessons did you learn after your first promotion into managing people?

Reinhard: My first promotion into management was at BMW as the Manager of Network Development and Distribution position. Before that, I was in an analytics role at BMW. My most significant learning was the role switch from doing analysis to leading people. After the promotion, I stayed heavily involved in analytics as I was good at it and enjoyed it. I soon realized that my role is much different now; it is less analytical and more communicative within and outside my department. My responsibility is to motivate my team members and provide them political coverage. I know and can do the work, but I must allow my employees to do the job. So they can learn and grow.

Madan: What triggered these lessons?

Reinhard: My boss noticed that my relationships within the organization were deteriorating and recommended that I work with a personal coach. The coach helped me understand that a new skill set is required to manage people.

A skill that I needed to learn. As a manager, my role is more of a coach and motivator; that is, I help my employees do their best job.

Madan: How did you apply these leadership lessons as you took on more responsibility?

Reinhard: I learned I could have a more significant influence developing and using 'Personal Power' versus relying on my 'Position Power.' I implemented an open-door policy. They can come to me with any problem. I'd listen, and jointly, we will devise a solution. I did not want to keep my distance as a leader. We developed close relationships. Yes, that made it difficult to deal with a problematic issue. I will have an honest discussion. The employee understood the situation and appreciated the feedback. This approach to building mutually trusting relationships also worked with my boss. We could have a frank discussion in our one-on-one meetings, which he appreciated.

As a young guy, I was impatient and would get upset if someone did not understand my idea. Now, I take a step back and try to understand the other person's point of view.

I came to the U.S. with BMW, and after three years, Audi approached me to join their organization. I found that every company has its own culture and language. Even the exact words have different meanings. I made it a point to adapt Audi's culture and language.

To help my employees develop strategic thinking skills, I schedule one-hour meetings with no fixed agenda. We discuss general things about what is happening in the larger business environment, not just the automotive area. Everyone is encouraged and expected to share information. I listen to them, and there is complete freedom to present ideas.

We are working on a 2030 shared vision for North America regarding transitioning from Combustion engine to EV (Electric Vehicles.) This shared vision encompasses the strength of our brand, the future portfolio, and how we get from here to there.

Madan: Is there anything else you want to share that has been the key to your career success?

Reinhard: First, take on a job out of your comfort zone or areas of expertise. Taking on a new area awakens my natural curiosity and creativity. Five years ago, my boss said, "Can you assume responsibility for Audi Training?" This is training the people working in the dealerships. I don't have any experience in training, but I said, "Yes."

Be open with people. I told them I needed to learn more about the training area and asked them to help me. People love to educate and help you if you ask them.

Recently, I was asked to be the Chief Digital officer for North America. Again, I still need an IT background, but I love learning new things.

I'm asked to take on more responsibilities because I have built a reputation for delivering results. My boss does not need to follow up. He knows I'll come back with a plan and execute it successfully. So, build a reputation for 'Delivering Results.

CHAPTER 7

Relationships, the Key to Tapping People's Creativity and Commitment

"But to lead, being smart isn't sufficient. You have to connect with people, so that they want to help you move the organization forward." (Robert Joss - Dean, Stanford Graduate School of Business)

The growth potential of a business is measured by the quality of its relationships with its stakeholders. One of the significant components of Business leadership is relationships. Relationships play the single most crucial role in you being a successful 'leading for innovation and growth' leader.

– Company's relationship with customers

– Management's relationship with employees

– Relationships among peers at all levels of the organization

– Relationships among various functions

– Relationships among people within a department

– Relationship with stockholders/investors

– Leader's relationship with self

Leadership is an extension of you, the analytical you, the emotional you, the human you with human needs. How these needs are being met determines your relationship with yourself and others. Unmet needs do not go away. They create conflicts internally and get in the way of you being an effective leader. Chapter eleven is dedicated to leader's relationship with self.

Our relationships play the most essential role in manifesting success and happiness in life, both on and off the job. The growth of a business is determined by the quality of its relationships with its customers and associates. A professional's development and career success are determined by the quality of their relationships with their staff, peers, and superiors.

Analytically, 1+1 equals 2.

In relationships, however, 1+1 can be more or less than 2

How - you may ask. To answer this, reflect on just two of your many work relationships. Pick one in which you look forward to working with a person and feel completely free to share ideas, however wild they may seem. Pick another where you dread meeting someone and do not feel free to voice your opinion. What is the crucial difference between these two relationships? In one, you feel secure, and there is mutual respect. In the other, these feelings are missing.

"If you have an apple and I have an apple, and we exchange these apples, then you and I will still each have one apple. But if you have an idea and I have an idea, and we exchange these ideas, then each of us will have two ideas."

— George Bernard Shaw

I was once conducting a leadership workshop for Human Resource managers in Chicago. I asked the 30 participants in attendance, "We have had several bosses throughout our careers. We didn't care much for some bosses and would be happy when it was time to go home. But for some bosses we liked and respected we would go an extra mile. What was the difference?"

One of the participants, Marsha, raised her hand and said, "*I would walk over hot coals for my current boss.*" I requested her to elaborate on why. She replied, *"I'm a single mother of two daughters in school. Sometimes, I need to attend a meeting at school or take them for a doctor's appointment in the middle of a workday. He gives me the flexibility to do that. I have happily worked many weekends to make sure he is successful."* What made the difference for Marsha? It was the feeling that *my boss cared about me*. The feeling that *my needs matter*.

Ben is the owner and president of a small service company. I have been consulting with him for some time and met him recently. During our meeting, Ben shared that he had visited a customer the day before, who said, *"Ben, we are delighted with the service your team provides. What else can you do for us?"* The feeling of trust between these two parties makes their association a business growth relationship.

Positive Feelings that Nurture Relationships 1 + 1 > 2	Negative Feelings that Undermine Relationships 1 + 1 < 2
Trusted	Distrusted
Secure	Insecure
Appreciated	Unappreciated
Respected	Disrespected
Recognized	Ignored
Acknowledged	Overlooked

Figure 7.1

1+1 > 2

There is extra energy, collaboration, and joy to be found in relationships nurtured by positive feelings. Employees in trusting relationships choose to give the gift of their discretionary effort – their commitment and creative ideas. Trust and respect are the foundation of any relationship. If I feel respected, then I will feel free to come to you with my concerns and ideas.

Respect and trust create positive energy. All of us have a need to love and be loved. And we love to feel good about ourselves. Appreciation from those we love and admire can have a very energizing effect. And naturally, having tasted the heady feeling, we are drawn to people who make us feel good about ourselves.

Employees who are committed to their leader and organization bring greater energy to their jobs. They are motivated to go the extra mile to satisfy customers with an *absolutely, positively whatever it takes'* attitude. I witnessed this attitude several times during my rides with FedEx couriers in Hongkong, Tokyo, Mumbai, and Helena. James Briscoe, one of the couriers, said – *"I treat my route as if it were my own business, and if I were running a business, I'd want customers to feel they were dealing with somebody who is friendly, professional, and helpful."*

1+1 < 2

We see depleted energy, avoidance, and disappointment in relationships undermined by negative feelings of being unappreciated, insecure, or ignored. Employees in distrusting relationships withhold their discretionary effort.

If we love those who make us feel good, isn't it natural to avoid those who make us feel bad?

PERSONAL POWER IS STRONGER THAN POSITION POWER

In the true sense, power is the ability to *influence* others' behavior, not to control, change, shape, or manipulate it. Blain Lee writes in *The Power Principle: Influence with Honor*, "Power is something other people feel in your presence because of who you are, what you stand for, and where you are going."

Position power gets you compliance. Personal power (through trusting and caring relationships) brings you commitment and creativity. For business growth in today's highly competitive economy, an organization needs people focused on designing and delivering a superior customer value proposition. In organizations where leaders rely on position power, most employees' energy is diverted to pleasing the boss instead of serving the customer.

Leaders who rely on personal power to influence people operate with a script – "My role is to serve you, the people who serve the customers." They let employees know that "I'm here to support you, so all your energies are devoted to serving the customer – the boss, who writes all of our paychecks." They are *Servant Leaders*. The Servant Leadership theory was introduced by Robert

Greenleaf in his book *Servant Leadership: A Journey into the Nature of Legitimate Power and Greatness*, published in 1977.

Robert developed his theory of servant leadership as an executive at AT&T. He got the idea of *The Servant as Leader* after reading Hermann Hesse's *Journey to the East,* a story about a band of men on a mythical journey. One of the novel's central figures is Leo, a servant who accompanies the party and does their menial chores but also sustains them with his spirit and song. He is a person of extraordinary presence. All goes well with the party until Leo disappears. Following this, the group falls into disarray and abandons their journey since they cannot make it without him. After years of wandering and decline, the narrator – an original party member – finds Leo and is taken into the Order headquarters that had sponsored the journey. He finally discovers that the *servant* Leo was the head of the Order, its guiding spirit, and a great and noble *leader.*

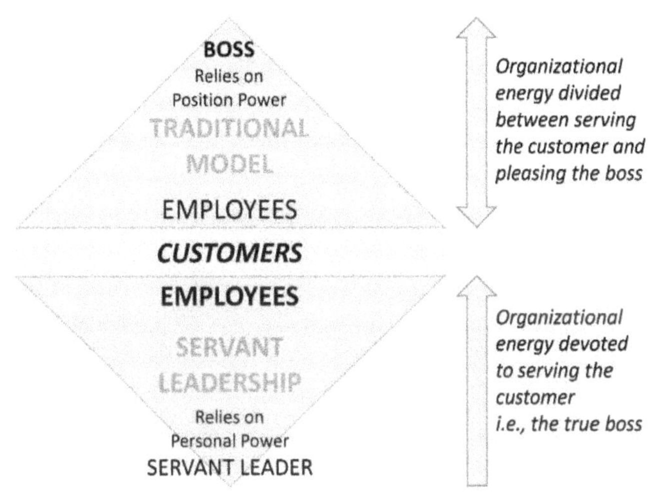

Figure 7.2

The typical organization chart shows the boss at the top and customer-facing employees at the base. In this setup, where the boss relies on position power, part of the employees' energy is spent on pleasing the boss. The servant leadership philosophy flips the pyramid upside down. The boss is at the bottom while customer-facing employees are at the top. The boss focuses on serving the employees who serve the customers. Here, the boss relies on personal power – sustained by caring and supportive relationships.

CUSTOMER IS THE BOSS

In 1989, as part of a new international expansion strategy, FedEx acquired Los Angeles-based Flying Tigers, an all-cargo airline. To welcome Flying Tigers employees into the FedEx family, founder, and CEO Fred Smith flew to Los Angeles, where many Flying Tigers employees had gathered before a small stage in the company's vast 747 hangar at LAX. Behind the stage was a tall backdrop with a large arrow pointing down and 'The Boss' printed in bold letters above it. As Fred took the stage, that arrow pointed right at him. As is common among employees of any acquired company, the audience was already apprehensive, and the sign did not help. They probably thought, "*Yes, we know you're our new boss. You don't have to flaunt it.*" However, Fred stepped aside without saying a word and peeled away a large sheet of paper taped below the arrow, revealing the word 'Customer' in bold in large print.

Fred then spoke to the gathering, beginning his remarks with these words, *"The only 'boss' at FedEx is the customer. I'm not the boss. I'm here to support you, the people who serve the customer. You maintain, load, and unload the airplanes. You pick up, sort, and deliver the shipments..."*

His entire talk emphasized the centrality of the customer at FedEx and the imperative that every employee maintain a laser focus on meeting customers' needs.

BUILDING 1+1>2 RELATIONSHIPS AT WORK

"Personal relationships are the fertile soil from which all advancement, all success, all achievement in real life grows."

— Ben Stein

One of the great joys in my life is my time on college campuses, having conversations with students. I usually start my talks with the question, "Who here would like to travel all over the world and let someone else pay for it?" Of course, everyone in the class raises their hands. I'll SHARE THE SECRET WITH YOU since I did that at FedEx and continue to enjoy it after retiring. The two factors that helped me win successive promotions and allowed me to retire early were *ideas* and *relationships*. In other words – *creativity* and *collaboration*. Chapter six discusses both in detail. In this section, I share other leaders' and my experiences building 1+1>2 relationships.

For any business, meeting its customer's needs requires all organization functions to work together, as no singular function can do its part effectively without collaboration and support from other departments and teams. As Managing Director of Materials Planning and Long-Range Planning at FedEx, my departments and staff worked closely with at least seven departments. One of the things I could do to help my team do their jobs better was to build relationships with the other departments. When we talk about building relationships with other departments, we are talking about building relationships with the people who work there. Below are some practical ideas that will work equally well for building relationships within and outside your department.

The following quote from Oprah Winfrey's speech to Harvard grads beautifully summarizes the key to building mutually trusting relationships. "*The common denominator that I've found in every single interview is that we want to be validated. We want to be understood.*"

Remember To Share the Stage

Every month at FedEx, Fred Smith chaired meetings of the Long-Range Planning Committee. In most of these meetings, my group was on the agenda. I started every presentation by acknowledging the contribution of other departments and, whenever possible, made joint presentations with my collaborators. I was in that role for ten years. A few years into it, I started asking my managers to attend the monthly meetings with peers from other departments they were partnering with when we discussed their projects. This experience helped them develop better presentation skills and self-confidence, and the exposure to senior management helped with their career growth. Four of my managers received promotion to managing director positions in other parts of the company.

Adam Bryant interviewed Gordon Bethune, CEO of Continental Airlines, in January 2010 for his column *Corner Office* in The New York Times.

Q. What are the most important leadership lessons you've learned?

A. I was a mechanic in the Navy, and mechanics in the Navy are like mechanics in airlines. You may have more stripes than I do, but you don't know how to fix the airplane. You want me to fix it? You know how much faster I could fix the airplane when I wanted to than when I didn't want to? So, I've always felt that if you treat me with respect, I'll do more for you.

As I went up the ladder in the Navy, I never forgot what it's like to be down the ladder and that being good at your job is predicated pretty much on how the people working for you feel. Here's my theory: Let's say we're all midlevel managers, and one V.P. slot is going to open up. I've got ten guys working for me, and for the last five years, every time I got any recognition, I said, "Bring them on the stage with me." Who do you think is going to get the job? I'm going to get the job.

Keep Your Door Open and Listen

When I became a manager at RCA, I quickly noticed that people loved working for my boss, Dale. The reason was that his door was always open, not just for his direct reports but for any employee in the organization. He did not try to solve every problem right away but asked questions and listened actively. People always left his office feeling that they were understood.

The June 2022 issue of TIME magazine was titled 'TIME 100' and featured short stories on 100 influential people the magazine was honoring. In one of these stories, John Mather, a Noble laureate and NASA astrophysicist, wrote the following piece on Gregory L. Robinson, Program Director for the James Webb space telescope – "*Greg is our program director at NASA headquarters, and to build such an engineering marvel and scientific success, he channeled the forces of human nature and ingenuity: NASA, the U.S. House of Representatives and Senate, the European and Canadian space agencies, Northrop Grumman, the launch-vehicle company Arianespace in France, and the Space Telescope Science Institute, where we command the telescope. Our teams orbit around Greg because we trust him to ask questions, understand our concerns, and respect our opinions. He makes it look easy, but I can barely imagine how he does it, and I admire him tremendously for it.*"

Another thing I found very useful was visiting my staff in their offices and cubicles – a less hierarchical setting. I would ask them how things are going. When you are interested in what people think and feel, they're more likely to connect with you.

Make Your Expectations and 'Why' Clear, But Don't Tell Them How to Do It

Delegation is one of the most essential tools in a manager's toolbox. Delegating tasks frees leaders to devote their time and energy to higher value-adding activities. People want to know what they are doing and why they are doing it. Effective delegation provides both responsibility and freedom. People want autonomy – to know *I'm in control of my work*. The feeling of control allows them to use their creativity in deciding how to accomplish a task. I have often been pleasantly surprised by my teams' better solutions than I had in mind when delegating a task. It is the only way employees can grow and gain self-confidence.

If a manager runs everything, the top talent will try to get out, while the bottom talent will let him do all the work.

Praise in Public and Criticize in Private

This rule sounds obvious, but we have all seen it violated repeatedly. FedEx had a recognition program called *Bravo-Zulu* or *B.Z.* where employees got a letter spelling out a specific above-and-beyond effort with a 'B.Z.' sticker. Also included would be a reward with some monetary value, like a gift certificate for a nice restaurant in town.

I learned the proper way to reward B.Z.s from one of my peers, the managing director of one of the departments we served. He would request a five-minute slot in my staff meeting to publicly announce the Bravo-Zulu award whenever a staff member from my department would win one for going above and beyond their regular duties. At times, they would invite the awardee to their staff meeting. People proudly put framed copies of these awards at their work desks.

I have observed that when people receive no reward, praise, or encouragement for their work, they eventually stop caring about whether or not they are doing a good job. Another thing I'd like to point out is that for special recognition, you should not hesitate to ask your boss or other senior members of the organization to present these awards. I found that senior leaders would happily oblige whenever available – all I needed to do was schedule my staff meetings to suit their calendars.

Tell Your Staff the Importance of Their Role and The Difference They Are Making

People need to feel that their role is essential in life and on the job. Tell them precisely how their work makes the company's customer value proposition superior to the competition. People sometimes need help understanding how the company makes money, so they may not fully visualize how their work fits the big picture.

Another thing employees like is hearing about the big picture from senior management, things like the company's profit outlook for the current fiscal or the organization's growth strategy. When Jeff was promoted to senior vice president of my division at FedEx, he became my boss' boss. He came from Finance and was very interested in getting up to speed on the operational and engineering details of the department he now led. Whenever he attended a meeting near my office, he would stop by to talk about my group's projects. I chaired a monthly meeting of Long-Range Planning directors and their managers, so I asked Jeff if he could join those meetings and share the big picture with us since that would be greatly helpful to our strategic planning." Not only did Jeff agree to join the monthly meetings, but he often stayed back to listen and participate in our discussions. He ensured to clearly explain to the attendees the importance of the work they were doing.

Texting, Zoom, and FaceTime are not substitutes for face-to-face meetings when building relationships.

Text, email, and collaboration software like Zoom and Microsoft Teams are undoubtedly helpful tools; however, $1+1>2$ relationships demand more than that. They have an emotional connection element. As I have said earlier, people connect with people at the feelings level. In-person, face-to-face meetings let us know people as their 'whole person.'

As mentioned before, my department worked closely with seven other departments. I requested my secretary to ensure I was scheduled for lunch with my counterparts in each department at least once a quarter. In those lunch conversations, in addition to work topics, we learned about each other's families, hobbies, favorite restaurants, sports teams, and more. These exchanges helped create a comfort level where even the wildest ideas would get a fair hearing. The collaborative environment we built at our level as directors served as an example to the managers and team members working under us.

Ken, one of my bosses at FedEx, would sponsor a friendly barbecue competition every summer in which teams from various departments participated. In addition to the participating teams, leaders from each department, managers, and vice presidents attended the event. The games and cooking contest allowed people across the organization to interact in a fun environment. Face-to-face interaction is a critical component of building trust, and events like this go a long way in building many relationships.

As leaders, we hesitate to ask for help, afraid that it is a sign of weakness, a blow to the ego. On the contrary, asking for help makes you human and brings you closer to others. People have a psychological need to feel needed. When you ask someone for help, you meet this need – they feel valued. It is always much easier to ask for help in a face-to-face meeting.

MY EXPERIENCE, UNDERSTANDING AND OBSERVATION OF EGO'S ROLE IN RELATIONSHIPS

A balanced meal is a healthy meal. A balanced lifestyle is a healthy lifestyle. Balance is the operative word in nature as well. Plants and animals only thrive when they exist in a balanced environment. I believe a balanced ego – neither weak nor strong – is a healthy one.

Figure 7.3

People with a healthy ego are confident in their abilities. They display an 'I can' attitude and are unafraid to take on new projects and greater responsibilities. They can trust people and form nurturing relationships. They are not dependent on constant external validation to feel good about themselves as opposed to a person with a weak ego. A person with a healthy ego enjoys quiet confidence fed by internal values and personal achievements.

In contrast, a person with an overpowering ego is fed by title, power, money, and possessions – external factors. The higher these people go, the more tightly they wrap themselves in 'position power' and the less comfortable their subordinates are to share bad news with them. Arrogant leaders with unhealthy egos demand respect, while secure leaders with healthy egos are servant leaders and are respected naturally.

Leaders With Healthy Egos are Learners

The ego is the most dangerous thing for an artist. That you start believing in your grandeur, that's the end of your creativity.

—Marina Abramovic

In The New York Times, October 29, 2023

People with an overpowering ego believe that they know everything, while people with a weak ego fear that by asking questions, they will reveal to others that they don't know something. People with a healthy ego feel secure internally, so they learn to listen and ask questions. They operate with a growth mindset. They don't shoot the messenger. They apologize when they are wrong. They give credit where it is due. They let go of control and let others lead whenever possible. They accept others as they are and let them grow differently. They step out of the spotlight and let it shine on others. They take genuine pleasure in the success of others.

On the other hand, people who often use *I* and seldom say *we* are insecure and will have a hard time when challenged. An unhealthy ego does not want to be better; it only wants to be seen as better.

Unhealthy Ego Makes Everything Personal

"Growth begins when we start to accept our weakness." Jean Vanier

When I honestly look back at the most disturbing interpersonal conflicts I experienced on and off the job, it is clear that they were all a consequence of my unhealthy and overpowering ego, which made the other person's behavior personal to me. It made me overlook that the other person was sharing their opinion or concern about something I had done and had nothing to do with me. Even with all this knowledge and understanding, I find that the ego is always in play, so keeping the unhealthy ego under control is a lifelong task. The more we get into the habit of placing ourselves in the other person's shoes, the better we get at letting a healthy ego drive our behavior.

"If you are willing to look at another person's behavior toward you as a reflection of the state of their relationship with themselves rather than a statement about your value as a person, then you will, over a period of time, cease to react at all." (Yogi Bhajan)

Ego is the number one killer of good decision-making within organizations. Teams work better when the team members check their egos at the door. A small amount of time devoted to building relationships pays big dividends in becoming an inspiring leader.

"A book to help readers understand the importance of managing/prioritizing relationships with subordinates to maximize their discretionary effort will be helpful. While it seems obvious to all of us (after all, most all of us have, or have had, a boss and are well aware of what motivates us, what angers us, what gives us pleasure/joy, etc.), the reality is that it is difficult for leaders to find/make/prioritize the time to do it effectively in a high-stress environment where so many left-brain deliverables are expected and are often overdue.

The good news is that small amounts of effort/progress in this area usually generate immediate improvements in staff goodwill and satisfaction. The results can be dramatic if one invests only 5-10 minutes daily on such matters. I am unaware of other literature on this topic, but your book can contribute to the literature on this critical matter."

— Graham Smith,
Former Senior Finance Executive at FedEx

"I realized that the fear of failure was driving my choices. A lightbulb turned on — my valued added role as a manager is not 'doing the work' but 'enabling the people on my team,' i.e., moving from a doer to an enabler." A conversation with **Kelly Dowdy, VP of Global Digital Commerce at Yum! Brands**

Kelly joined Boeing as a software engineer after completing her undergraduate work in Information Technology at Carnegie Mellon. During the 11 years at Boeing, Kelly progressed from software engineer to the CIO's chief of staff and finally to executive director of technology. During this time, she also completed graduate work in Information Systems at Carnegie Mellon. After a successful tenure at Boeing, she joined Express

Scripts as a Senior Executive Director. Currently, she is the Vice President of Global Digital Commerce for Yum! Brands, the subsidiaries of which include KFC, Pizza Hut, Taco Bell, and Habit Burger Grill.

This conversation occurred while we waited for a delayed flight to New Delhi, sitting in the American Airlines lounge at JFK airport.

MB: What changes did you have to make when you first moved from an individual contributor role to managing people?

KD: For the first nine months, I was involved in the details of every project my team worked on. A lead engineer in the department told me, "Get out of our sandbox. Here is what we need from you: remove the roadblocks. That will enable us to be more productive and do a better job."

That made me reflect on my behavior and my choices about allocating my time and energy. I realized that the fear of failure was driving my choices. A lightbulb turned on – my valued added role as a manager is not 'doing the work' but 'enabling the people on my team,' i.e., moving from a doer to an enabler.

I started spending more time communicating and connecting with stakeholders, building relationships down, across, and up the organization. I spent more time talking to team members and influencing them.

I started to view my role as standing up on a balcony and watching the people dancing on the floor (i.e., people doing their work), letting them tell me where they need my help, going down to the floor, and without stepping on their toes, help them and get back to the balcony.

MB: What would you say have been the keys to your success?

KD: 1. My learning agility – I did not realize I had that; my mentors noticed it. I had just moved into the VP role. Six months later, I was asked to apply for a Senior VP position. I told the person, "I'm not qualified. I just got here."

A few weeks later, I made a presentation to senior management. The global CIO was impressed and pushed me to go for the position. "You have been in three different industries and have made a difference in each one. You will do well in the new position, too."

2. My way with people, i.e., building trusting relationships. I love people and make it a point to spend time with them. I talk to them about things outside work. I now believe what others see in me. Three people from previous organizations followed me to Yum!. I don't know all the technical details, but I fully trust my people.

IV

Developing and Unleashing Yours and Team's Natural Innovation Skills

"One of the most coveted human skills is creativity, and this won't change. Machines will enrich and augment our creativity, but the human drive to create will remain central. In an interview, novelist Jhumpa Lahiri was asked why an author with such a special voice in English chose to create a new literary voice in Italian, her third language. "Isn't that the point of creativity, to keep searching?"

— Satya Nadella in his book "Hit Refresh'

We don't have to force the mind to think creatively because the nature of the mind is to think. It's thinking all the time. We just have to provide the right conditions for the mind to engage in generating creative ideas.

CHAPTER 8

How to Generate Creative Ideas

"Thought, not money, is the real business capital."

— Harvey S. Firestone

Unleashing your team's and your natural creative potential

The nature of the mind is to think. That's what the mind does; it's thinking more than one thing at a time. Creative thinking is 'what-if' thinking, connecting dots (knowledge) in imaginative ways that have never been connected. What if we make this change in our business strategy, product design, manufacturing process, distribution process, billing system, and accounting system?

"What if there is an airline dedicated to flying critical, time-sensitive packages?" was the subject of a college term paper by Fred Smith while he was studying at Yale. This idea led him to start FedEx.

The thinking, "What if we typed using only our thumbs?" by Mike Lazaridis led to the birth of Blackberry.

The thinking, "What if there was a video rental service similar to a health club?" by Reed Hastings led to Netflix.

What if thinking by Larry Page, Google's Cofounder, was the genesis of Google and continues to be its growth driver.

*"One night I had a dream (literally) and woke up thinking...**what if** you could download the whole Web and just keep the links? So, I grabbed a pen and scribbled down the details to figure out whether it was really possible. The idea of building a search engine wasn't even on my radar at the time. It was only later that Sergey and I realized ranking web pages by their links could generate much better search results."*

— Eric Schmidt & Jonathan Rosenberg

In *How Google Works*

"The creation of something new is not accomplished by the intellect but by the play instinct from inner necessity. The creative mind plays with the objects it loves."

— C. G. Jung,
Renowned Swiss Psychiatrist, 1875-1961

Creativity is the generation of novel/new ideas by:

- Connecting dots, making connections between seemingly unrelated variables.

- Imagining things in a fresh light.

- Questioning current assumptions.

Innovation is the generation, acceptance, and implementation of creative ideas. It is people who come up with the ideas, and people from all impacted areas – collaborating with each other – develop and successfully implement these ideas. Successful execution is the great differentiator in our global economic competition. A brilliant idea may be destined for trouble without brilliant execution. **Innovation needs both creativity and collaboration.**

Great Ideas (Creativity) + Great Execution (Collaboration) = Great Results

Generating creative ideas is the first step in the three-step innovation process. Step two is gaining acceptance of the idea and collaboration from people in all impacted areas. Innovation is a people process and a team sport. You must be effective in a team setting to be a great leader. In a TIME magazine interview, the former Lockheed Martin CEO, Norman Augustine, shared, "Most innovation today involves large teams of people. We have to emphasize communication skills, the ability to work in teams and with people from different cultures."

Bill Watkins, CEO of Seagate, shared with Newsweek, "A company like ours is all about teamwork, people being able to make decisions for the betterment of the team over their department, division, or organization. I've found that people learn best when I put them in a situation that they're not comfortable in, where they've got to learn to ask for help, and they have to learn to make decisions together."

You don't have to have all the dots in your head. Team members can build upon each other's ideas. Creative ideas are generated when regular, thoughtful people work with other regular, competent people and combine ideas in original ways.

We don't have to force the mind to think creatively. **If the mind is healthy and growing, it will produce creative ideas.** We must provide the right conditions for the mind to generate innovative ideas. The fantastic thing is that you don't have to try hard to be creative – it just happens naturally and automatically. Following are the four conditions represented by the acronym MINT:

Mint v. To coin, to invent, to forge; to fabricate

(The mind fabricates ideas from knowledge, the available raw material.)

Mint n. A source of abundant supply

(With its imagination capability, the mind has an unlimited capacity for generating ideas.)

Webster's Dictionary

MINT

Four Conditions For The Mind
To Generate Creative Ideas

Figure

More Dots	Imagination	Nominal Stress	Time
Knowledge Base	Right Brain Thinking	Creative Tension	To Explore What-Ifs

8.1

Tim Berners-Lee, Web founder, after winning the first Millennium Technology Prize, shared, "I was just taking lots of things that already existed and added a little bit. Building the web, I didn't do it all myself,"

Berners-Lee took concepts well-known to engineers since the 1960s, but he saw the value of marrying them. He fleshed out the core communication protocols needed for transmitting Web pages: the HTTP, or hypertext transfer protocol, and the so-called markup language used to create them, HTML.

More Dots

The more dots your mind has, the more connections it can make. And the dots do not have to be all from your field. More innovations come from connecting dots from disparate fields. Examples of the Mind Connecting Dots in Imaginative Ways to Solve Problems from my book, 'Unleashing Creativity and Innovation: Nine Lessons from Nature.'

What if there was a video rental service similar to a health club? Solution: Netflix

I had a big late fee for "Apollo 13." It was six weeks late, and I owed the video store $40. I had misplaced the cassette; it was all my fault. I started thinking, "How come movie rentals don't work like a health club, where, whether you use it a lot or little, you get the same charge?"

— Reed Hastings,
CEO, Netflix

What if there was a card that could be used as cash? Solution: Credit Card

In 1950, Frank McNamara found himself in a restaurant with no money and came up with the idea of the Diners Club Card. The first credit card changed the nature of buying and selling throughout the world.

Management Review, November 1998

What if there was a clean, friendly, and moderately priced accommodation for a traveling family? Solution: Holiday Inn

When the Wilson family of Memphis went on a motoring vacation, they discovered it was not much fun to stay in motels that were either too expensive or too slovenly. So Kemmons Wilson built his own. The first Holiday Inn opened in Memphis in 1952.

Management Review, November 1998

Curiosity Preceded Creativity

More Dots Your Mind Has, More Connections It Can Make

"The creative person wants to be a know-it-all. He wants to know about all kinds of things: ancient history, nineteenth-century mathematics, current manufacturing techniques, flower arranging, and hog futures. Because he never knows when these ideas might come together to form a new idea. It may happen six minutes later or six months down the road. But he has faith that it will happen".

Carl Ally, responsible for the innovative and memorable ads that helped FedEx become a household name

Imagination

Imagination is the right brain asking "what if" by connecting dots in imaginative ways, as reflected by Einstein's quote, "Imagination is more important than knowledge. Knowledge is limited. Imagination encircles the world." During creative thinking, the mind is in a playful mode, playing with dots, its knowledge base.

"There is no question that a playfully light attitude is characteristic of creative individuals."

— Mihalyi Csikszentmihalyi

If you want to see Imagination in action, just watch children at play.

"I get my innovation inspiration from children. They have an amazing ability to change ordinary objects into whatever they need them to be by using their Imagination. They have the ability to see beyond what is in front of them and create new uses for items. I marvel at how my children can turn a bedroom into a sea. The bed into a pirate ship, pillows into sharks, and empty paper towel rolls into swords."

— Jamie Woolf,
Learning and Development Specialist, Kimberly-Clark

What happens to our Imagination as we grow up? Creativity, the process of connecting dots in imaginative ways, gets blocked because we were trained to come up with one correct answer during our high school and college years. Just because you have not exercised your Imagination lately does not mean you have lost this incredible capability. It's waiting to be unleashed. Remind yourself and trust that creativity is, in fact, the true nature you were born with.

Nominal Stress (Creative Tension)

A violin cannot play a sweet note unless the strings are under pressure. But if you put too much pressure on the strings, they snap. So do we. When the violin is not being used, you release the tension on the strings. We too need periods of relaxation to recover and renew.

— Tanya Wheway

Similarly, the mind needs creative tension. Creative tension is the gap between where we are and where we want to be.

How often have you come out of the shower with a solution to a problem on your mind? You had a good night's sleep and were relaxed in general. In this state, the neurons played around and made new connections to resolve the tension. For the mind to create new connections, it needs to be in a playful mode.

An overly stressed mind is not in a creative mode. When under stress, the neurons take the path of least resistance – the known pathways. When facing change, the response becomes, "This is how we've always done things around here." An overly stressed mind says, "Don't talk to me about the future. Let me get through today."

George Ballas was experiencing creative tension from trying to mow his tree-packed lawn. To solve this problem, he created a prototype Weed Eater from a tin can and fishing wire.

The role of leaders is to set specific goals for improving business processes, cost structure, customer experience, and so on; the goal is a stretch, far enough to require greater effort but not too far away to be unattainable. This leadership practice creates the necessary creative tension and starts the creative problem-solving journey.

Time

Creative problem-solving requires time to engage the mind in exploring "what if" before locking into "how to." Also, it takes time to develop a raw, creative idea and get it ready for implementation.

Where is the time to think if you're constantly running from one meeting to another? Your busy calendar must reflect a balance between doing and thinking by scheduling some quiet time to think. For example, Intuit, an accounting and financial software provider, gives its employees 10% of their hours as unstructured time, time to think creatively about improving Intuit products and services.

Schedule quiet time for creative thinking by turning off all electronic devices.

"Don't check your e-mail when you're creating. Nothing earth-shattering is going to happen in an hour or two."

— Anna Rabinowicz,
O Magazine, Feb. 2011

CHAPTER 9

Gaining Acceptance of Your Creative Ideas

"Only a baby with a wet diaper likes change."

— Mike Ullman,
Former CEO of JC Penny

Innovation is the act of introducing something new. That means change, giving up the old ways. A creative idea is life-altering; it threatens status-quo. It brings about changes, and even though the need for change is understood intellectually, it is uncomfortable emotionally.

President Woodrow Wilson once said, "If you want to make enemies, try to change something."

A few years ago, I got a call from the CFO of a large financial services company, asking to meet her. In our meeting, she shared that she had just added their corporate IT department to her portfolio. She said, "The IT team does a good job supporting day-to-day operations and does what I ask them to do. I want them to innovate because, in Financial Services, IT is not just a support function; it is a key part of the company's customer value proposition. Can you work with my senior managers in developing 'Leading for innovation and growth' leadership skills?"

During my one-on-one meetings with the managers, I heard this statement repeatedly: "Madan, I have ideas that would improve our processes and save lots of money, but the Operations people just don't understand." They could not gain acceptance of their ideas from the people responsible for the implementation.

I asked one of the team leaders to walk me through his approval-seeking process. He would make a PowerPoint presentation with a thorough analysis and flow charts. Operators would share a concern and ask a question. He would respond with another slide full of data, but it would fail to satisfy the operators. He had been working on the idea for six months, was convinced it would work, and could not understand the resistance.

The problem was not his analysis but a fear of the unknown on the part of the operators. They had genuine concerns about whether the idea would work on the shop floor as advertised. What the operators were looking for was the 'feeling of being understood' – being shown that their concerns were understood and appreciated. Our technical backgrounds orient us to data and logic so much that when asked to recognize feelings, we struggle as if trying to make sense of a badly out-of-focus picture.

"In the modern business world, it is useless to be a creative thinker unless you can also sell what you create."

— David Ogilvy,
Founder of Ogilvy & Mather
And known as the "Father of Advertising"

A few years ago, I was invited to speak at Google. I gave them a list of topics to choose from to be sure I would address their needs. The topic they chose was, 'How to Gain Acceptance of Your Ideas.' We want not just 'acceptance' but 'wholehearted acceptance.' It is natural for problems to crop up during implementation – foreseen or not – that the implementation team must address. Wholehearted acceptance of an idea means a commitment to it, and committed people will find a solution when faced with a problem.

"One person with passion is better than 40 people merely interested." **– E.M. Forster**

Gaining acceptance is a people process and requires effective communication and people skills. The first step is to understand why people resist change. Resistance can be tough to identify for technical/analytical professionals in engineering, finance, information technology, and others.

Why do people resist change?

There are many reasons why people resist change. The following are the most common ones.

1. Different view of the world than the idea presenter: The person who implements the idea is responsible for day-to-day operations and delivering the product on time. The idea presenter works in information systems. The operations manager is genuinely concerned and unsure if the idea presenter understands the operational nuances.

2. Fear of change and unknown: Anything creative results in change. People know how things work now but have yet to learn how they will work in the future. Fear of the unknown is a major cause of resistance because the unknown is unpredictable. They sense the risk of the unknown whenever you push past the current envelope of people's experiences.

"It is important to remember that the fear of change rather than the reality of change is the real culprit. As the French philosopher Michel de Montaigne noted, "My life has been filled with terrible misfortune, most of which never happened."

Alina Tugend,

The New York Times, March 20, 2015

3. Why didn't I think of it? The person feels that he should have come up with the idea. He feels his stature and value in the organization will go down. Other people will get the credit, and there is only so much credit to go around.

4. Vested interest in maintaining the status quo: The current process was designed by him. It's his baby. It works. Even good change threatens familiar routines, policies, and comfort zones. It's normal for people to resist change and push back toward the familiar, especially when the old method of doing things benefits them. NBA once resisted the 3-point shot.

The above shows that resistance is a reaction to an emotional process in the person resisting your creative idea. **You cannot persuade people out of how they are feeling through logic and data.** But that's what we do when we pull up another PowerPoint slide to share more analysis. The overriding need of a person feeling the fear of the unknown is to feel that you understand his concern. You have heard the expression, "Deal with the people where they are."

Visualize this: You are standing on a staircase and looking five steps up where you see a bright future after your idea is implemented. The operations are more efficient, product quality is much better, employee productivity is higher, and so on. The people who will implement your creative idea are on the steps below where you stand. You want them to climb the steps with you to a bright future. They cannot see the bright future and must be motivated to reach it. You must reach down and ask the person to trust you and hold your hand. Help the person climb up to where you are standing.

Now, you both see a bright future and with this shared vision, you start climbing and reaching the desired state.

Here is another example of dealing with people where they are. You are ready to go to work. You drop your two-year-old daughter at the daycare on your way to work. She is crying because her favorite doll's plastic hand is broken.

Scenario one: You tell her, "Stop crying. Daddy will get you a new doll." You think it's only a few dollars, and I'll pick one up after work. She does not stop crying and is not ready to leave home. She feels terrible because the doll, her baby's hand, is broken, and the doll's mom, your daughter, feels her baby's pain. You could forcibly strap her in the car seat and head to work. She cries all the way to the daycare. You feel bad.

Scenario two: You say, "Oh, I can see your doll's hand is broken. She is hurt and must be feeling bad. Let us see what we can do to fix her broken hand." You get some tape band-aids and fix her hand with your daughter's help. She stops crying. You suggest, "Let's put the doll in the crib. Ask her to kiss the doll and cover her with a blanket. She needs to rest and will recover when we get home." She gets in the car, and you drop her at the daycare after a peaceful ride.

The acronym for the model we'll discuss for gaining acceptance is ELSE.

Ask: Who ELSE do I need for successful implementation?

As I said earlier, we need not just acceptance but wholehearted acceptance, the key to successful implementation. When people are committed wholeheartedly to the idea, they passionately engage in successful implementation.

"There is a mistake technical and scientific people make. We think that if we make a clever and thoughtful argument, based on data and smart analysis, then people will change their minds. This isn't true. If you want to change people's behavior, you need to touch

their hearts, not just win the argument. We call this Oprah Winfrey rule."

— Eric Schmidt & Jonathan Rosenberg
In *How Google Works*

ELSE

Four People Skills Required for Gaining Acceptance of Your Creative Ideas

Figure 9.1

Expect and Respect Different Perspectives

The people affected by the change you are proposing have different perspectives on the situation because of their knowledge, experience, interests, and areas of responsibility. Those perspectives must be respected. Once the mind is prepared to hear different views, it does not become defensive.

Have you noticed the reflex when a baby smiles back at its mother? This reaction is mirror neurons at work. Mirror neurons help in intuiting other people's intentions to feel their pain. Mirror neurons re-create the experience of others within us. We start to feel their actions and sensations in our minds as if we were doing these actions and having those sensations.

When you walk into the meeting, seeing others as reasonable, rational human beings and accepting different perspectives, your reaction to their resistance/concerns will reflect respect versus frustration. After confidently sharing your idea, you invite others to do as well. If you are open to hearing others' points of view, they'll be more open to yours. People's mirror neurons will see and mirror your positive response. When others feel respected and trust your motives, they let their guard down and begin to listen. The most potent way to win opponents is to accept their concerns as legitimate, which triggers an instinct to reciprocate.

I started the chapter by discussing my consulting assignment on coaching I.T. executives on this skill. When someone raised a concern about their idea, the response I suggested to them was, "That's a very important point. Bill, you know more about the operations than I'll ever know. I need your help to make sure I fully understand your concern. I'm not clear on please tell me more."

Listen to understand versus listening to respond.

Typically, when someone is talking about his concern about the idea, the presenter's mind is thinking about the response and what he is going to say instead of listening to fully understand his concern. The most profound human need is 'I matter.' That means my concerns matter. When others listen to my concerns, I feel valued. As discussed earlier, even though people may understand the general need for the change, they will probably feel uncomfortable. Those feelings need to be acknowledged and recognized. The only path to validating their feelings is by listening to understand versus listening to respond. It means listening to the words and the emotions behind them. The marker for this skill is not that we feel that we heard but that the other person feels understood.

Steven Ballmer, Microsoft C.E.O., interviewed by Adam Bryant, New York Times, May 17, 2009

"Q: Are there areas you want to improve as a leader?

A: I race too much. My brain races too much, so even if I've listened to everything somebody said, unless you show that you've digested it, people don't think they are being well heard. Sometimes, you really don't hear because you're racing. It's just the way my brain works. My brain is just chop, chop, chop, chop, chop. And so, if you really want to get the best out of people, you have to really hear them, and they have to feel like they've been really heard. So, I've got to learn to slow down and improve in that dimension."

- The words LISTEN and SILENT have the same letters. For listening, the mind has to be silent and free of noise/internal chatter.

"Andy and I are currently researching the neuroscience of interpersonal dialogue, and we know that effective communication requires deep listening. Deep listening requires exquisite silence. Until we master this skill, we can't be wholly present nor listen fully to what the other person says and feels."

—Mark Waldman, Loyola Marymount University, and Andrew Newberg, MD, Jefferson University Hospital.

- As technical/analytical professionals, we also need to recognize that logic can convince, but only the feeling of being heard and understood helps gain whole-hearted acceptance of our ideas. Are you a literal listener? After watching me communicate with one of my employees in a meeting in her office, my boss commented, "Madan, you are a literal listener. You're not fully comprehending what Lisa is saying. You need to also listen to the feelings behind her words."

- Confident people are thoughtful and good listeners. They value outside opinions and consider them carefully. I've found that the ideas shared in these conversations often lead to making the original idea better.

Jana Eggers is the C.E.O. of Spreadshirt, a maker of personalized clothing (T-shirts with sayings) with offices in Boston and Leipzig, Germany. In an interview with the New York Times, she shared the following. "I have another one that stirs up quite a bit of controversy: a Madeleine Albright saying – "Be confident, not certain." And it's funny to me how many people don't like that: "Well, what do you mean? If you're not certain about it, you're supposed to be confident about it?" And again, it goes back to listening. When you're certain something is right, you get blinders on."

- Finally, growing up in another culture and working with people from around the world, I found that, at times, words and gestures mean and convey different things. We assume that others have had our experiences, and that's how we listen to them. We need to be sensitive to diverse cultural backgrounds.

"I need to let people talk in meetings. Otherwise, why do I have those people? And I need to see who can make a decision and who can contribute. We have all this instant communication now. What I've learned from my experience working in Japan, Korea, and other Asian countries is that they've been around for thousands of years, and they will take their time. And if you're going to be successful in that part of the world, you'll have to develop patience."

— F. Mark Gumz,
President and C.E.O. of the Olympus
Corporation of the Americas

Speak their language

At the FedEx Leadership Institute, we discussed keeping the letters SAP in mind while preparing and making presentations. The letter S stands for Subject. What's the Subject of your presentation? Letter A stands for Audience: Who are you making this presentation to? Letter P stands for Purpose: What's your purpose in making this presentation? Get approval for your idea to proceed. Get funding? Get feedback? F.Y.I., status update? Gain acceptance of your creative idea, including their support and involvement in implementing it.

Every function or department has its own vocabulary, priorities, knowledge, and experience base. It would be best to incorporate the function's language while presenting how your idea will benefit them, make their life easier, and help them achieve their goals.

"Each emergency was a drill held by the Defense Advanced Research Projects Agency (Darpa), the Pentagon's moonshot research arm. Its goal was to expose utilities accustomed to dealing with hurricanes, blizzards, and other challenges to the reality of a successful cyberattack on the U.S. electrical grid...

The 100 or so participants in each drill spent a week to 10 days. Employees from utilities and people from National Guard units role-played at their day jobs while Darpa brought in cyberwarfare experts to act as the hackers. The biggest challenge was a culture clash between seasoned utility operators and experts in cybersecurity. "You have to get your systems operations guys, who don't speak cyber, to talk to your cyber guys, who don't speak system operations. And that's just very challenging." says a consultant."

— Bloomberg Businessweek, January 31, 2022

When the audience is senior management, use 'Business instead of Functional' language: When you're in the trenches or playing a highly specialized or technical role, it's easy to fall into the trap of using technical or functional language in selling your ideas to senior management. Avoid that at all costs. Instead, speak their language and explain how your ideas will help them reduce costs, increase revenue, and improve the company's value proposition as it enhances the customer experience. If you're asking for resources, you should build your presentation around how your idea and the resources will ensure the successful execution of the company's business growth strategy.

Expand the ownership of your idea.

Just think about how excited you are in ensuring the idea is implemented successfully if you were involved in developing the idea. You are expanding ownership by engaging people with concerns or reservations about the change you are proposing in exploring creative solutions to the problems raised. Better yet, identify the people you will need for its implementation and who this idea will impact. Approach them one-on-one with, "Susan, I've been thinking about this idea and need your help to see if it has any potential. You are good at looking at the big picture." Making someone feel important is an excellent way to get support. Being informed and engaged makes it easier to accept.

"Ask for help and encourage involvement. It's pretty hard to dislike someone or not want to build a relationship when the other person says, "I could use your help." "What do you think?"

— Bill Repp,
Management Consultant

A T.V. host was interviewing me on one of my books. During the break, he asked me, "What do you do when the other person takes credit for your idea?" Drawing upon personal experience, I said, "Don't worry about who gets the credit initially. Management will determine who had the original idea once it's successfully implemented and producing results."

How do you expand ownership?

1. Solicit and incorporate their ideas

"The strength of a project team lies in its members' ability to build on one another's ideas – especially the half-baked ones. But the best collaboration is rooted in trust, which comes from a shared experience that binds colleagues together." **— Ivy Ross,** Mattel

2. Present jointly to senior management and acknowledge all team member's contribution

If one or two people are critical to successful implementation, co-author the proposal and present the idea jointly. Like the Oscar winners, give credit to everyone you talked to and the key to successful implementation, "I want to thank …. For their valuable contribution in developing this idea."

3. Make it their idea

Author Steven Levy shared the following story with the NPR reporter Laura Sydell. John Doerr, an early investor in Google, said to Google founders Larry Page and Sergey Brin that you need to hire a C.E.O. (adult supervision). Larry and Sergey went back to the office and called back to say we didn't need one. Instead of saying I'm not going to fund, John said, "Just go and talk to a C.E.O. you admire." Larry Page and Sergey Brin interviewed Eric Schmidt. At that time, Eric was chairman and C.E.O. of Novell, a software Services company. Before that, he spent 14 years at Sun Microsystems, starting as a manager and rising to Chief Technology Officer. Impressed by him, they recruited Schmidt to run their company.

John met Larry and Sergey where they were and worked with them to let them make it their idea.

"A dream you dream alone is only a dream

A dream you dream together is reality." **— Yoko Ono**

As mentioned earlier, my group developed package sorting hubs and airport expansion plans to support FedEx's growth strategy. Fred Smith, FedEx C.E.O., wanted the regional vice presidents responsible for operating these hubs and airports to present these plans rather than us, the planners. He wanted the operators to understand in detail as they were critical to the successful execution of these plans. Throughout the planning process, my engineers have been working with regional engineers. We would fly out a week before the Long-Range Planning Committee's meeting to the regional office for detailed reviews and help the vice president finalize his presentation.

Gaining acceptance and securing collaboration is a process and not an event. It takes time.

"You will observe with concern how long a useful truth may be known and exist before it is generally received and practiced on."

— Benjamin Franklin

Remember, the relationships you've been building play a key role in opening ears and hearts to gain acceptance and develop your ideas. Relationships, more than information, determine how ideas get accepted and implemented. Cultivate your relationships with influential people before you need them.

CHAPTER 10

Developing Your Strategic and Business Thinking Skills

As mentioned in the first chapter, for any organization to grow in today's fast-changing business environment, its internal rate must exceed the external rate of change. A long list of companies once sat at the top of their fields but have since fallen by the wayside because they needed to recognize or keep up with changes in the external world. They were far too focused internally and ended up paying the price. Every organization will be impacted by changes to their environments from a growing list of sources – technology, customer needs and expectations, competition, supply chain, government regulations, the global economy, climate change, workforce availability, and demographics, to name just a few.

Regardless of how bright a CEO is, one person cannot keep up with all the changes. Every manager must 'look out the window' and contribute their observations to the organization's strategy development process. External changes present both opportunities for and threats to growth.

"I want the people running the business to be strategic planners. Part of the responsibility of a business leader is to be a strategist. I want to know what the competition is doing, where we're ahead, where we're behind, and what we will do about it." (Larry Bossidy, CEO of Allied Signal)

LOOK OUT THE WINDOW:

THE FIRST STEP IN DEVELOPING BUSINESS STRATEGY

I consulted on strategic planning at Smith & Nephew a few years ago. In the first meeting, the company's president, Larry Papasan, shared his philosophy with me, "There is a reason the windshield of a car is much larger than the rearview mirror. To reach your destination, you must look through the front windshield at the big picture and what's happening down the road. You don't go forward and make progress by looking in the rearview mirror."

Suppose the external world – your larger business environment – is not changing. In that case, you can continue to do what you are doing, maintain your market share, and grow at the general rate of growth in your industry. But things in the world are changing, and the rate of change is accelerating. The role of business strategy and strategic planning is to ensure that the internal rate of change is greater than the external changes. Many environmental factors affect all businesses across the globe. Let us look at some of these factors.

Technological Advancements

Technology is the most significant ongoing change and presents a huge opportunity to gain a competitive edge. At FedEx, I frequently heard senior management say, "FedEx is a technology company that happens to have airplanes, trucks, and sorting hubs." Indeed, the extensive application of technology-enabled FedEx to sort and track packages, manage the supply chain routes, and optimize their operations to the maximum. In the 21st century, every company is a technology company, and all business processes rely heavily on technology. Advancements in areas like cloud computing, artificial intelligence (AI), the Internet of Things (IoT), robotics, machine learning, and more require businesses to constantly adopt new technology to stay ahead of the competition in meeting customer expectations. We have seen how technology has played a central role in creating and growing new business models in e-commerce, social media, mobile banking, ridesharing, and others. The following is an example of technology's role in agriculture, an industry most only sometimes consider.

"Robots are also moving into agriculture as vision and machine learning improve. Stout Industrial Technology Inc. in 2020 began selling a machine that's pulled by a tractor and weeds large fields. The machine's sensors distinguish between a desirable crop and the unwanted weeds after being fed thousands of photos to teach it the difference, and the device chops down the weeds with a hoe-like blade. This is usually backbreaking work done by crews of about 25 people." (Bloomberg Businessweek, April 4, 2022)

Here are four 'Looking Out the Window' activities that have helped me, and many others keep up with the changes in the larger business environment.

Ongoing in-person conversations with vendors and suppliers. My peers and I found that these conversations in our conference rooms or at vendor sites were very helpful in learning about new advancements in technology and their applications. The foundational ideas for numerous projects at FedEx came out of these general information conversations and saved the company millions of dollars.

Attending tradeshows, conferences, and user forums. The key benefit of attending tradeshows is seeing a wide assortment of technology and equipment under one roof. My first job after college was working as an industrial engineer supporting manufacturing, warehousing, packaging, and distribution at RCA. I made it a point to attend the American Management

Association's packaging show in New York. The successful application of manufacturing and packaging automation ideas picked up in those tradeshows not only helped me reduce costs and improve customer service but also resulted in special recognition, pay raises, and promotions for me.

Read professional and business magazines. In addition to reading professional and technical journals, I made a point to read Businessweek, Fortune, Fast Company, and TIME magazine. These journals and magazines provide a big-picture view of the current economy and insight into future trends.

Take advantage of seminars and classes offered by universities. As mentioned earlier, my preferred learning method is college classes and books. When I went to college, all of my learning was on mainframes. When minicomputers were introduced in the late seventies, I was curious about their capabilities and applications. I came across a brochure about a weekend seminar on minicomputers at Purdue University, an hour-long drive from Indianapolis, where I lived. The exposure in that class allowed me to work on a minicomputer-controlled automated pick-and-pack system for RCA Music Service. That project got me promoted from a project engineer to manager of warehouse distribution systems.

Changing Economy and Customer Expectations

In the 1950s, if someone wanted a birthday cake, they would have to go to the grocery store, search through different aisles, buy the needed ingredients – flour, butter, sugar, etc., and bake a cake from scratch. It was a **commodity economy** back then. Since all grocery stores stocked and sold these commodities, competition kept the profit margins low. Someone thought, *"What if we put all the needed ingredients in a box so people wouldn't have to walk all over the store? Plus, the ingredients will be in the right quantity to bake a cake."* Betty Crocker introduced a new product – cake mix in a box – and ushered in a **product economy**. Since the cake mix in a box made it more convenient to shop and bake, that added value allowed charging a higher price than the cost of individual commodities. It moved up the value chain.

Then someone thought, *"With both husband and wife working, they are pressed for time. What if they ordered the cake to be ready on the desired day? They can pick up the cake on their way home."* The neighborhood grocery store and the corner bakery started offering this service, so it became a service economy. They could charge even more since they eliminated preparation and cooking from the customer's process. Of course, people who wanted could still bake one from scratch or use a cake mix, but increasingly, more people favored the **service economy.**

Then someone else thought, *"If you don't want a group of five-year-old kids running all over the house at your child's birthday party, then bring your group to our location. We'll have a cake, birthday hats, entertainment, pizza, and children's games. The children will have a fun experience."* Chuck-e-Cheese pioneered this concept, and with their model, it became an **experience economy.** They could charge customers more since they added more value than just a pre-made cake.

Yet another genius thought, *"Your daughter enjoys playing soccer. What if you bring your group to our club? We will have a cake, hats, drinks, pizza or other food items from our menu, soccer balls, and shirts customized for each child with their names. The kids will play soccer in our indoor field before cutting the cake. They will go home with a soccer ball and custom jersey."* Since the club was customizing the experience, they could charge more, and the product moved further up the value chain, an example of a **personalized experience economy**.

You can see a similar value progression in all sectors of the economy – dining, vacations, wedding planning, home building, meetings/event planning, software, and so on. Your business customers' needs are changing because the business model is changing. Companies must continually enhance their products and services, customer experience, and value proposition to maintain a competitive edge.

Because of the wide selection to choose from, consumer goods brands need to connect with their target customer at a deeper psychological level. They need to respect and acknowledge the customer's emotions, such as the yearning to belong, the need to feel connected, and the desire to experience joy. Innovative companies recognize that great products and services can deliver more than profits; they provide experiences that make life better in a small, tangible way.

Visit Customers to Understand Their Changing Needs and Expectations

Software Users. Brad Smith is a former CEO of Intuit. Under Smith's 11-year run as CEO, he transformed Intuit from a North American desktop software business to a global cloud product and platform business with well-recognized offerings like QuickBooks, TurboTax, and Mint. Several years ago, he shared Intuit's *'Figure Out the Customer'* process in an interview.

First, we break the company – which has 8,000 employees – into four to six-person teams. We call them "two-pizza" teams because you don't need more than two pizzas to feed them. They observe the customers. They watch someone in a coffee shop, they watch someone at the florist, they follow farmers home, and they look for big problems that are getting in their way. Then they come back to the office and come up with at least seven different ways to solve that problem. No idea gets scratched off until they run an experiment to see whether the customer likes it. And the ones that work the best are the ones we build products behind. We get a lot of neat ideas this way [Brad Smith, Fast Company].

Changes present opportunities for growth as well as threats to existing businesses based on how organizations respond. Here is an example of how one well-established consumer products company first ignored the changing needs of its customers. Then, after seeing threats to their business, they changed their product portfolio.

Consumer Goods and Changing Lifestyles. This interview with the CEO of P&G's grooming arm was published in the May 16, 2022, issue of Bloomberg Businessweek.

More than half of men now sport beards, including two-thirds of millennial men. The groupthink among marketers in the grooming division was that facial hair would be a short-lived trend. That stoicism proved catastrophic. Gillette was selling an aging line of products to a shrinking audience instead of innovating in lockstep with the lumberjack-chic look prevailing among actors, athletes, musicians, cover models, online influencers, baristas, bartenders, and oh, almost any man from Shoreditch in London to Silver Lake in Los Angeles regardless of how the crow flies.

In 2019, with Gillette's revenue catering, P&G wrote down the value of the brand by $8 billion. In 2020, it rolled out a line of face washes, shave gels, combs, waxes, oils, and beard-friendly razors named for founder King C. Gillette. Reimagining Gillette for the modern man is one of the toughest challenges in the consumer goods industry [Gary Coombe, Bloomberg Businessweek].

During COVID, most Levi's stores worldwide were closed, and revenues dried up. The company's CFO, Harmit Singh, shared with Bloomberg Businessweek how Levi's adapted to this big external change. "First, we pivoted to a new strategic blueprint based on three things: elevation of the brand, acceleration of our direct-to-consumer business, and diversifying our product base. We just closed a deal and entered the athleisure segment with Beyond Yoga. Younger consumers like products that are more sustainable. And that means that you've got to go back and make a change in your closet, and you need to engage with brands that are engaging you." (Harmit Singh - CFO of Levi's, Bloomberg Businessweek)

Climate Change

Climate change is imminently going to impact all industries, directly or indirectly. It's not something that is 20 or 30 years away. The once every 100-year floods, forest fires, droughts, and heat waves are happening worldwide. Nations all over are scrambling to develop plans to reduce their carbon emissions.

Inward-looking leaders are poorly equipped to confront the risks of climate change. Category 5 hurricanes are wreaking havoc on housing, infrastructure, supply chains, and insurance costs. Higher temperatures reduce labor productivity and put stress on power plants to keep up with the increased demand. Tesla isn't alone; all auto companies are moving towards electric vehicles.

Melting ice feeds rivers that supply water for agriculture, households, and industries. Less ice on the mountains means less water downstream. No sector will be able to sidestep the impact of these changes.

Global Economy and Global Supply Chains

During my tenure at FedEx, the company organized an annual officers and directors' meeting at an offsite location. The purpose was to review the company's current fiscal year performance and strategic growth initiatives for the coming year. These meetings provided an excellent opportunity to meet colleagues from around the world. In addition to presentations from our CEO and other senior officers, there was also a talk delivered by a guest speaker, usually a CEO of another company. At one such meeting, Michael Dell, founder and CEO of Dell, was the guest speaker and shared, *"The Dell desktop computer was conceived in Texas; it consists of a frame built in China, a screen made in Taiwan, a microprocessor designed in Oregon, memory chips produced in China and assembly work done in Malaysia, with the software sent over from a Seattle suburb. The whole unit was shipped back to the U.S. on a jumbo jet built in Washington State and operated by FedEx, a company in Memphis, Tennessee."*

Numerous other products we use every day, such as mobile phones, home appliances, clothes, and cars, have similar global supply chains. All parts of any supply chain have to work perfectly to make a product available on time and meet the customer's needs at a reasonable cost. We have had supply chain disruptions before, but nothing on the scale and duration like the one brought on by the COVID-19 pandemic.

The global economy is here to stay because the customers and suppliers are international, and materials are also sourced globally. However, the most recent prolonged disruption has caused companies and countries to rethink and redesign their supply chains. At FedEx, engineers are assigned to every sales team to understand the customers' business and help customize supply chain solutions.

FROM FUNCTIONAL TO BUSINESS ORIENTATION

For the successful execution of a corporate growth strategy, each function – product development, supply-chain management, manufacturing, marketing, sales, information technology, distribution, or customer service – must develop a plan that aligns with and supports the corporate strategy. As technical professionals, our systems approach to problem-solving and desire to keep up with changes in our fields provide an excellent foundation for developing strategic planning skills. In a functional orientation, the system is viewed as a function, but in a business orientation, the system is the business, and the picture is bigger.

In one of his books, Daniel Goleman shares the findings of a study that involved executives at fifteen large companies. "Just one cognitive ability distinguished star performers from average: pattern recognition, the big picture thinking that allows leaders to pick out the meaningful trends from a wealth of information around them and to think strategically far into the future. These star performers relied less on deductive, if-then reasoning and more on the intuitive, contextual reasoning characteristic of a symphony."

Shifting from a functional orientation to a business orientation takes some effort. One needs to do several things:

- Learn every little detail of the product or service your company sells

"Whatever your product is, make sure everyone in the company understands the product. We have every employee on their first day make a vacuum cleaner – even if you are working in customer service."

— James Dyson,
Inventor of bagless vacuum cleaner

- Understand how your organization makes money, your customer value proposition, and how it differs from the competition

- Learn all business processes, not just those of your department

During the Christmas season, FedEx's package volume doubles. The Memphis hub, the largest hub in the system, hires and trains thousands of seasonal workers to handle this increased volume. The week before Christmas is the busiest period of the holiday peak season, and for just that week, hub management requests volunteers from other Memphis departments. Throughout my ten years in Materials and Resource Planning, I volunteered to work in the hub every year. This firsthand experience gave me detailed knowledge of hub operations and helped me build great relationships with the managers and directors there.

At that time, I had no idea that in my next position, I would lead a team responsible for designing hubs worldwide. The operational knowledge and relationships I built volunteering for the peak season made this transition much easier.

- Learn how 'what you do' helps your organization meet your customers' needs. Specifically, what elements of the value proposition do you directly impact?

After the peak season one year, I had a chance to spend some time with Karl, vice president of the Memphis hub. The hub's primary goal is to launch cargo flights on time so teams in the destination cities can deliver packages before the promised time. Karl told me that he holds his managers accountable for the launch and the package delivery service level in the destination city. *'Did the customer get the package on time?'* This action encourages his managers to work closely with their peers in the city stations.

"According to former employees, Starbucks keeps two chairs empty at every meeting or conference - one for the customer and one for the employee. They are meant as a constant reminder not to give shareholders outsize consideration." (Bloomberg BusinessWeek, August 2, 2022)

- Step out of your silo to understand how your process impacts other business processes

- Understand how – by working together – you can improve these business processes

- For communicating with senior management, learn to speak the business language in addition to functional language

Think and speak in terms of how an idea could impact the bottom line. You will often notice that people in Finance departments grow and get promoted faster than other functions. This happens because of their job demands' bottom line and business orientation.

Speaking from a deep understanding of a subject is crucial to effective leadership. Learn as much as possible about your company and industry (including best practices and trends) and determine how to use that information effectively. Make sure to present information and add insights to it. Think about what business insights any piece of information provides.

Gary Bronson, a Principal Advisory Consultant in Amazon Web Services (AWS) and former VP of IT Operations at FedEx shared the following personal experience of how he helped his teams move from a functional orientation to a business orientation.

"As IT professionals, we often can become isolated from the business/customers and may lose sight of key business objectives and priorities. I have always focused on understanding the core business and the 'intended' culture (often, sub-cultures creep in and must be avoided). That positions me to learn the importance of strategic initiatives and the overall vision of business leadership. Once obtained, I work to ensure that every person in the organization has total transparency to what I'm aware of related to that topic.

An example of how this solved a critical business problem was while I was at FedEx, we were working to transition the necessary workload from one platform to another.

The team supporting the 'legacy' platform was highly dedicated, knowledgeable, and talented but had yet to be engaged in any of the work supporting the strategic direction.

The leadership accountable for the transition was explaining that the lack of visibility to specific business processes created a high-risk situation for the transition and that we needed to know when data was being 'screen scraped' (a process of grabbing the information showing up on the screen and routing it to a file for future use) and how it was being used. I debriefed with a group of our technical team supporting the legacy environment and allowed them to sit in on one of the sessions. After just one session, they went offline and, within 24 hours, had an idea to resolve the problem. Within three more days, they had a prototype. Within a few weeks, they had the solution up and running, which provided transparency to each officer for their respective areas. It also offered the specifics so targeted actions could occur to learn about the necessary business processes and established controls so alerts would happen when new efforts occurred.

The team continued to mature the solution with additional reporting and received numerous accolades from all the leadership that benefited from their solution.

They were energized and saw that their value to the business was much more than supporting a legacy platform."

CREATIVE STRATEGIC PLANNING STARTS WITH 'WHAT-IF' THINKING

Creativity is thinking *what-ifs* to imagine something different and better. It involves connecting dots (your knowledge) in ways they have never been connected. In the business world, this translates to generating creative ideas that can improve your organization's product quality, cost of doing business, or customer experience. As mentioned earlier, the successful implementation of a corporate strategic initiative requires each function to develop and implement its supporting initiatives. I remember back in the 1980s, as part of a business growth strategy, FedEx launched a corporate initiative called '*Get close to the customers.*'

In those days, shippers needed to fill out an airway bill to ship packages via FedEx. Shipments with multiple pieces required them to fill out multiple airway bills. This shipping requirement could have been a better experience for commercial customers. These were pre-internet times, and as part of getting close to the customers, someone in the IT function conceived this idea – *"What if we place personal computers in customer warehouses to generate airway bills?"* This action would speed up a highly time-consuming and tedious task for customers and eliminate the manual process within FedEx to enter shipment information into tracking and billing systems. The warehouse computers would be connected to FedEx systems, and a separate department called 'Customer Automation' was created to develop and implement this initiative. The computers were periodically upgraded with new functionalities like electronic billing, package tracking, and more to improve the customer experience.

Every business has customers that generate large, medium, and small revenues. FedEx customers range from large volume multi-national shippers to single package walk-in customers. A proposal from the Customer Service function said, *"What if we assign a dedicated group of customer service agents to each large shipper so that when someone from a specific customer's office calls, they will be routed to an agent familiar with their account? The terminal can automatically display the account information. The agents would even know the caller from the customer's office as they would talk frequently."* This functional initiative not only resulted in expediting the answering of customer inquiries but also helped FedEx get closer to the customer by developing relationships.

The Sales function suggested, *"What if we hire logistics and supply chain professionals in the Sales department to work with account executives? These experts will work with the account representative in developing and presenting customized supply chain solutions to help the customer enhance their business value proposition."* This elevated FedEx from a supplier to a business growth partner.

The sorting system at FedEx's Memphis hub has miles of conveyors that carry packages from inbound airplane unloading to automated sorting to outbound airplane loading. Packages that exceed specific dimensions and cannot travel on the conveyors are designated non-conveyable and must be sorted manually. The manual sorting operation was slower and sometimes resulted in delaying outbound flights. Corporate Engineering established a packaging department to consult with customers to redesign their packaging for automated sorting. I remember how this team worked with several flower shippers to help redesign their boxes. Those redesigned packages were cheaper than the customer's previous packaging and ensured that all Mother's Day flower shipments were processed and delivered on time.

At its core, business orientation is customer orientation, as the purpose of any business is to attract and retain customers. Business thinking is customer thinking. If you don't consider your customers the reason for doing things, your business growth strategy will be in trouble.

V

Leadership is an Extension of You – The Human You

"You begin leading with honor by believing that you will never be more effective as a leader than you are as a person. Leadership is a journey toward wholeness. It is a journey that starts on the inside. As you align your values with your actions, you generate the personal power that enables you to help others do the same."

— Blain Lee,
The Power of Principle: Influence with Honor

Leadership is an extension of the total person– your knowledge, skills, worldview, attitude, feelings - the analytical you and the feeling you, the truly and completely human you with human needs. As a human, anything that impacts you, positively or negatively, also affects your leadership. To be the most influential leader, dare to be the most complete and balanced human being you can be. We become the human beings we can be by celebrating life in its fullness – a balanced lifestyle meeting all life's needs.

"At Harvard, the 180 spots in Prof. Arthur Brook's class "Leadership and Happiness" fill up quickly. Participants are taught how to cultivate their teams' happiness along with their own. A central tenet is that happiness is key to being an effective leader... popularity reflects both the demand for soft skills and students' desire for more balanced lives – and an intention among schools to turn out better bosses."

— **Lindsay Ellis**,

The Wall Street Journal, Feb. 14, 2022

CHAPTER 11

Leadership Excellence and Work-Life Balance/Harmony: An Energizing Relationship

(Adapted from my books 'Enjoy Balance and Unleash Creativity: Five Steps to a Happier, Healthier and Successful Life,' published in India, and "Balanced Life and Leadership Excellence: A Nurturing Relationship,' published in the U.S. and Germany)

I have given talks and seminars on this topic at Microsoft, IBM, Tata Consultancy Services, and FedEx, among others, and in Executive Education programs at Kellogg, University of North Carolina, Rhodes College, and others. Based on my experiences conducting this course, I published a book in collaboration with a psychologist.

A leader from Microsoft in Bangalore, India, called me, "Madan, we hire highly educated technical professionals from top colleges for innovative work, but after a few years, they are burnt out. Can you offer your workshop to this group?" Following the workshop at Microsoft, I facilitated workshops at several other large companies in India. An Indian publisher approached me to write a book based on my work in India. The book, 'Enjoy Balance and Unleash Creativity,' was published by Vishwakarma Publications.

Lessons that I learned and discussed in my workshops,

1. In today's highly competitive global economy, for companies to thrive, they must adapt and change. Creativity is the key to enterprise growth and career success in the 21st Century. Looking at life from the creativity and people skills dimension, career success and family life are mutually supportive.
2. We treat 'Work-Life Balance' as optional but pay a hefty price with what matters most – our health, relationships, and professional effectiveness, especially our creative problem-solving abilities and people leadership skills.
3. In today's fast-paced life, it is very easy to drift into an unbalanced lifestyle and only realize once it is too late that it is not the kind of life, we wanted at all.
4. Is it easy? No. First, there is no such thing as enjoying a perfectly balanced life every day. Is it possible? Yes, a reasonable balance for the majority of the time.
5. As we grow, we change. We assume different roles. Our life's needs change. Life is not a puzzle with only one correct fit. The puzzle pieces have to be taken apart occasionally and refitted together. Leading a balanced, harmonious life is an ongoing process.

Defining Work-Life Balance in the 21st Century

In the 20th Century, the 'Work-Life Balance' conversation centered on balancing the hours spent on the job with the hours dedicated to personal/family life – i.e., work from 8 to 5, and once home, detach from work and enjoy your personal/family activities. Today, with 24x7 connectivity, we no longer see a clear separation between 'work time' and 'personal time.' Smartphones, laptops, and other mobile devices make it very easy to receive and respond to work emails at any hour, from any place. That usually means checking on emails after the kids have gone to bed.

"Yet, when it comes to balancing work with family and personal life, he doesn't think our obsession with our devices is helping. He doesn't believe in work/life "balance" but in **work/life harmony.** There is no such thing as balance. It's how do I harmonize my work and my life?" - Satya Nadella, Microsoft CEO, quoted in the Times of India,

To better reflect today's inescapable reality of trying to fit together various life roles and responsibilities for success on and off the job, the American Psychological Association and the Society for Human Resource Management have started to use the term **'work-life fit.'**

While attending graduate school in Chicago, a church invited me to speak on vegetarianism. To help prepare for the talk, my roommate CK Shah gave me a book by the Jain *muni* (ascetic) Chitrabhanu. I liked Gurudeo Chitrabhanu's message and made it a point to visit his New York center during my business trips. He graciously blessed us with visits and talks in Indianapolis and Memphis. During one of our evening walks in Memphis, I asked him, "Gurudeo, what's the purpose of life?" With some reflection, he said, "The purpose of life is to celebrate life in its fullness." The derivation - 'Goal of balanced/harmonious life, is to celebrate life in its fullness' - became my guiding and operating mantra.

"What constitutes fullness?" We can view the constituents of fullness from many perspectives. One perspective is 'life roles,' i.e., balancing the limited time available to celebrate and enjoy all our life roles. The balancing process becomes increasingly demanding as more and more life roles are assumed – professional, manager, leader (career), spouse, parent, friend, mentor (People relationships), tennis player, gym partner, community member, etc.... Another term I've seen used is **'work-life integration.'**

When we choose well-being for the whole, the payoff is always greater. Multiple roles turn into multiple sources of joy. **Leading a balanced life is intentionally making choices that support wholeness and, therefore, celebrating life in its fullness.**

I'm a musician, but I'm also a father, a husband, a son, a citizen, an African American, an American – and at the root of all that, I'm a human being. My vision comes from my humanity, not from my being a musician. That opens it up and completely removes any walls.

— Herbie Hancock
Musician; Winner of multiple
Academy and Grammy Awards

My balanced life is a model for living that is based on positive assumptions about human growth and motivation. A balanced life can be visualized as a balanced, healthy state in which the individual uses all of their skills, takes charge of their life, and celebrates life in its fullness. The following Balanced Life Model incorporates the fundamental psychological concepts of human needs as motivators, the presence of an innate drive toward psychological maturity, and the importance of identity for psychological health and personal success.

People feel fulfilled when vital human needs are satisfied.

NEEDS	SOURCES OF SATISFACTION	SPECIFIC REWARDS
Recognition & esteem: I want to be somebody	Career	Power, social status, recognition, leadership opportunities, money.
Love & belonging: I want to be somebody to somebody	People	Mutual support, attention, affection, sexuality and sensuality, group membership, shared experience, communication.
Identity & self-respect:	Actualization	Realizing our potential Becoming the person we want to be. Reaching goals, we set for ourselves. Sense of meaning and coherence in life.
Physical & relaxation: "I want a break from living; recharging one's batteries.	Leisure	Activities chosen just for fun" and the pressures of being/ not for making a becoming somebody."

Figure 11.1

The psychological and human self is multi-dimensional. Each self has its own unique needs and makes a valuable contribution to our total happiness.

I have divided the pie into four pieces. You can slice it further into more details, e.g., the People Self can be split into various relationships, the Actualizing Self into volunteer, spiritual, and more subcategories that apply.

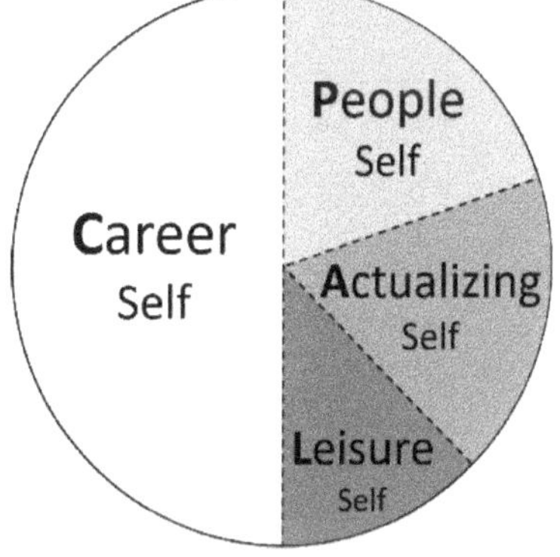

Figure 11.2

Living things in nature want to grow.

Just like plants and trees, growth is a basic human need. For an apple tree, the growth is sprouting a new branch. The branch becomes strong, growing a flower and then an apple — all manifestations of growth.

Similarly, children experience growth when they take the first steps or learn to say "mama" and "dada." As adults, we experience growth in the Career Self when we learn new skills or solve a challenging problem. We experience growth in the People Self by making new friends or existing relationships deeper. We experience growth in the actualizing Self when we grow spiritually. For example, we experience growth in the Leisure Self when we finally master that overhead shot in tennis or the chip shot in golf.

The growth need is met when a person does something or experiences something new. It does not matter to an apple tree that millions of other apple trees have produced apples. It is growth for the apple tree that it has grown and produces apples.

To live and grow requires an ecologically balanced environment.

The plants need a healthy balance of sunlight, water, and nutrition from the soil. Too much water and insufficient sunlight disturb the Balance and retard the plant growth. The simple act of moving the houseplant closer to a window restores the Balance and the growth.

We will discover that on and off-the-job roles may appear in conflict when viewed in isolation. Still, when considered as being integrated, they are, in fact, complementary C-PAL. Later in this chapter, you will see how a balanced life helps develop and unleash our creativity and people leadership skills.

Robert Gouizeta was CEO of Coca Cola from 1981 to 1997. Under his leadership, Coke's market value increased from $4.3 Billion to $181 Billion. Most afternoons, he headed home around 4:30 p.m., riding up front with his driver and listening to country music for a quiet evening with family.

When the ecological Balance is disturbed, the plants and marine life die.

We've all read how once-healthy lakes became polluted and the marine life disappeared. Or how, in some rivers or lakes where the marine life is not entirely dead, the growth has been retarded, and the size of the fish is much smaller than before. Similarly, our development as human beings is stifled when our lifestyle becomes unbalanced. The vitality and inner energy stop renewing itself, and we feel restless and tired. We go through the motions and may even have many external trappings of success but feel unfulfilled as human beings.

How Balance Helps in Developing and Unleashing Our Natural Creative Potential creativity: The key to enjoying a successful career

It creates the four conditions (MINT) required for the mind to generate creative ideas.

More Dots (**M** in MINT, the 4 Conditions for generating ideas)

A balanced lifestyle with time allocated for hobbies and new experiences helps create more dots, the first condition for making new connections. You're not shortchanging your career when taking time to pursue relaxing hobbies. A popular TV host, Dr. Phil, regularly advises the guests on his show, "You can't take care of others until you take care of yourself – you need Balance and joy in your life. Think back to a time before you became consumed by your job. What were your passions then? Did you enjoy jogging? Painting? Travel? Identify what excites and relaxes you, then make time to do it."

Human beings have habits that can be self-satisfying and self-fulfilling. An integral part of that habit is the development of hobbies. In the life of the average man, his wife and children, his work and financial position are central to his daily responsibilities and worries. Hobbies provide leisure and relaxation from the tenseness of more serious preoccupations. A significant source of unhappiness, fatigue, and nervousness is the inability to be interested in anything that's not of practical importance in one's life.

— Dr. Chulani,
Clinical Psychologist, Times Wellness, March 9, 2008

With their extended time for play, rest, and relaxation, vacations provide some distance to take in the big picture. We get an opportunity to reflect on what matters. The daily round is so assertive in its demands that we must consider the broader perspective of what we will do in the years ahead. We know what we want to be--a top-rate marketing manager, engineer, accountant -- but we still need to figure out how we want to spend our lives.

Every now and then go away,

have a little relaxation

for when you come back

to your work

your judgment will be surer;

since to remain constantly at work

will cause you to lose power

of judgment

Go some distance away

because the work appears smaller

and more of it

can be taken in at a glance,

and a lack of harmony

or proportion

is more readily seen

— Leonardo Da Vinci (1452-1519)

Reading, attending lectures, taking Classes just for the fun of it ... Be a learner

Our minds can only think to the breadth they are exposed to. So, expose yourself to as many fields as possible.

"And much of what I stumbled into by following my curiosity and intuition turned out to be priceless later on. Let me give one example: Reed College at that time offered perhaps the best

calligraphy instruction in the country. Throughout the campus every poster, every label on every drawer, was done in beautiful hand calligraphy. Because I had dropped out and didn't have to take the normal classes, I decided to take calligraphy class to learn how to do this. I learned about serif and sans serif typefaces, about varying the amount of space between different letter combinations, about what makes great typography great. It was beautiful, historical, artistically subtle in a way science can't capture, and I found it fascinating.

None of this had even a hope of any practical application in my life. But ten years later, when we were designing the first Macintosh computer, it all came back to me. And we designed it all into the Mac. It was the first computer with beautiful typography... Of course, it was impossible to connect the dots looking forward when I was in college. But it was very, very clear looking backward ten years later."

*— **Steve Jobs**,*
Stanford University commencement address

There is more to life than increasing its speed.

— Mahatma Gandhi

Ideas live in the realm of silence. They arise in a quiet mind. Ideas come to the person who is prepared to receive them. Slow down and be still for some time every day.

Imagination (**I** in MINT, the 4 Conditions for generating ideas)

Your imagination is a right brain capability. To unleash that part of your brain, find ways to:

- Actively pursue interests and hobbies.

"I really do get a lot of good ideas when I play horn. This type of meditation I'm describing is a very creative process. When I practice my horn, I don't look at music. I don't read a note. I simply play, I play melodies that come into my mind. I play scales.

I play slow exercises. I'll be playing my horn and all of a sudden, some business thought pops into my head. I'll go write it down. I don't know how to explain it, but that's just what happens."

— Jim Benham,
Founder of Capital Preservation Fund
and Performing Jazz Band

- Participate in and observe artistic endeavors – music, art, theater.
- Spend time in nature.

Writing books is both a left and right brain activity. My engineering education in India and the U.S. was entirely focused on developing and using analytical/left brain capabilities. Spending time in nature – hiking in the woods, climbing mountains, boating on the river, relaxing on the beach, and snorkeling in the ocean has been very helpful in developing my imagination/right brain capabilities.

"Apple is Tim Cook's life's work, and in this work, Tim displays mastery. Tim has demonstrated more range in his leadership of the world's largest companies than any contemporary CEO... Yet Tim does it with compassion and discipline, turning to nature to replenish spirit. In the summer he can be found hiking in our national parks, buoyed by the majesty of the mountains."

- Laurene Powell Jobs,
In TIME 100 issue, June 13, 2022

As difficult as it may be for some people to believe, relaxing is NOT a waste of time. Without proper rest, both your body and mind become exhausted, and your creative juices dry up. Adequate sleep, relaxation, and fun are a must for avoiding burnout.

How Balanced Life provides Inner Security to take risks in setting 'Innovation goals/Creative Tension (Nominal Stress)' (N in MINT, the 4 Conditions for generating ideas)

Someone who gets all of his kicks from work cannot afford to take any risk. Creativity means taking the risk in challenging the status quo. A balanced life celebrating life in its fullness does not put all eggs in the career basket. The multiple sources of joy are the foundation for feeling secure, a prerequisite for setting and achieving innovation goals.

As we discussed earlier, balanced life needs are not optional. The unmet needs stay. They create conflicts and stress. Setting and taking steps to meet PAL goals is the only path to reducing inner tension caused by expecting the job to fulfill emotional and spiritual needs.

The greater the congruence between inner wishes and conscious goals, the greater the available energy. To use my teacher's image, you must have both the bubbling up of thoughts and the capacity to release them. We all have, in varying degrees, this constant generation of images and ideas. The trick is to capture and harness them to make them work for us. Too much 'viscosity'--fear and unresolved feelings that oppose the effective expression of these ideas--can get in the way."

— Anna Fels, M.D.

Time to think (**T** in MINT, the 4 Conditions for generating ideas)

At lunch, I will go out and bike 20 miles. Then I'll get back, and all of a sudden, a thought comes to my brain, and I solve something I was struggling with. Goodnight (CEO of SAS) understands the innovative process, and there's time built for it.

— Mary Simmons,
Principal software developer, SAS,
FORTUNE, August 17, 2009

Edison's friends in Florida respected his need for privacy. He would go out to the end of his dock and sit and fish – but he'd fish without any bait on his line. Edison was not interested in catching fish; he was after time to think.

— James Newton,

Uncommon Friends, Harcourt Brace, 1987

Almost all technical, political, or social innovations come from thinking deeply about the subject. That means taking time to learn, think, and imagine. My favorite mini-vacations are long weekends on a lake or in the mountains. Recently, we rented a cabin on Lake Ouachita in Arkansas, a beautiful hideaway with woods surrounding the lake. In addition to being very relaxing, the hours spent on the cabin deck with the smartphone turned off were very productive in generating ideas for this book.

Taking a mandatory day off every week has done wonders for my productivity. I realized a few years back that I used to burn out every few months, and it was happening increasingly. By taking one full day off, I was able to give my body and brain a much-needed break that allowed me to come back to work refreshed.

— Apoorva Mehta, Instacart Founder

Fortune, October 1, 2015

Becoming an Innovation Leader

Whereas creativity deals solely with generating ideas by exploring "what if" scenarios, innovation starts with creative ideas but takes the process two steps further. Innovation does not just happen. It must be actively supported. Individual employee creativity is the first step of innovation. Managers/team leaders must create an environment where employees feel comfortable suggesting and experimenting with new ways of doing things.

An innovation culture actively promotes the three stages of innovation:

- Generation
- Acceptance
- Implementation

It's people who have creative ideas. It's people who accept and develop raw, innovative ideas. It's people who successfully implement the developed ideas. Leaders at all levels of the organization play the most critical role in creating and sustaining a supportive environment that actively engages people in the innovation process, developing and unleashing employees' natural creative potential at all levels of the organization.

In fact, about 75 percent of ideas that result in better products or services for companies come from front-line workers. When management finds ways to harness that creativity, firms reap benefits.

— ALAN ROBINSON,
Corporate Creativity:
How Innovation and Improvement Actually Happen

Interpersonal Skills and Intrapersonal Skills

A leader's interpersonal skills – how the leader relates to others to achieve common goals – are directly affected by their intrapersonal skills – how they relate to themselves. If he is not sensitive to his work-life balance needs, he will not recognize employees' need to have lives beyond work.

"Every person is a summation of various' selves.' If those units of the person are not in communication, then the person cannot maintain valid communication with others."

—Warren Bennis & Burt Nanus, *Leaders,*
Harper and Row, New York

"If you want to manage somebody, manage yourself. Do that well, and you'll be ready to start leading."

— John Zenger,
Leadership: Management's Better Half, Training Magazine

How unresolved life balance conflicts impact leadership effectiveness

A leader needs to solicit and listen to employees' creative ideas actively. If the leader depends on all their life's joy from their career, they will not take the risks involved in exploring new ways. Controlled by the unchecked ego, the leader thinks he has the correct answer; directed by this message, the mind stops looking for further information. The person stops listening and stifles creativity in the organization. A balanced life helps keep the ego in check.

Successful leadership presupposes having much of one's own psychological house in order. It becomes a tricky balancing act. These conflicts must be dealt with because they don't just go away if they're ignored. Suppressed feelings develop into compensating behaviors that are not conducive to effective leadership.

A Balanced Lifestyle with time for exercise keeps the mind sharp

Pumping up your body and mind with extra oxygen from exercise is the magic that gives birth to more brain cells and keeps the ones you have in top shape. It turns out that exercise is one key to "getting smart" and staying that way.

A morning workout triggers feel-good endorphins and lowers elevated stress hormones. The effects can last six to eight hours, says Gregory Florez, a spokesperson for the American Council on Exercise in Salt Lake City. "Morning exercisers tend not to have midmorning slumps and are sharper mentally than if they hadn't exercised." He says you'll get the most bang for your energy buck with a workout that includes cardio and strength training.

Time to Wake Up!
Real Simple magazine, May 2011

A balanced lifestyle with control of internet time frees time for what matters.

I have been thinking a lot about this. I work full-time and have a 1.5-year-old. I often feel that I've wasted away my day, but it is because I spend so much time on the internet. When I finally put away my phone and do something (cook, exercise, spend time with my husband, my hobbies!) I feel so much better. Check email here, Facebook, and Twitter there, and soon, we've been online for hours each day. I truly think that phones and the internet are sucking what we used to know as life away from us. Just like keeping a food diary often illuminates what we really are eating, keeping a time diary would show how much time we spend online.

— Anne from Chicago commenting on LAURA VANDERKAM's article 'The Busy Person's Lies' in The New York Times, May 13, 2016

Studies have shown that every time we interrupt what we're doing to check email, messages, Facebook posts, or the latest Twitter feed, it takes at least 15 minutes for the mind to get back to where it was before the interruption. The mind needs at least 15 concentration-filled minutes to get into the zone where it can think deeply and make new connections, i.e., think creatively.

Recruiting and retaining the best and the brightest

One of the critical responsibilities of a leader is to attract, develop, and retain the best and the brightest.

"Among women employees under 30 who were surveyed, nearly two-thirds said they would be more interested in advancing at work if they saw senior leaders exhibiting the kind of work-life balance the women seek for themselves."

"Companies that don't take action may struggle to recruit and retain the next generation of women leaders – and for companies that already have a 'broken rung' in their leadership pipeline, this has especially worrisome implications," the authors wrote.

The McKinsey/LeanIn.Org report is based on a survey of more than 40,000 employees from 55 companies, interviews with a few dozen survey respondents, research, talent pipeline, and other data from 333 companies. They represent over 12 million employees in the U.S. and Canada.

To meet the demands of being an effective leader, day in and day out, requires a lot of physical and mental energy, which means staying in good health.

In Sanskrit's ancient teaching and language, the word for health is "svastha," which means to stay in yourself. When we are in tune with the changing needs of our various selves (Career, People, Actualizing, and Leisure) and are leading a balanced life to meet those needs regularly, we enjoy health and come to work full of energy.

Health, happiness, and career success are the natural by-products of a balanced lifestyle celebrating life in its fullness.

A tiny, delicate flower may seem insignificant, but can color a hillside in sufficient numbers. Life's small pleasures and rewards can add up to a fulfilling life if repeated. Permit yourself to do what makes you and your loved ones happy.

The last chapter is a real-world example of 'Leading for Innovation and Growth.' Following is an example of a successful leader prioritizing work-life balance.

Chris Paul, an All-Star NBA player, talks about his mentor, Bob Iger, CEO of Walt Disney, in the April 4, 2022, issue of Bloomberg Businessweek.

"One of the most important lessons Iger taught Paul is work-life balance. It stuck with Paul that Iger once made a visit to Shanghai into a day trip so he could be back home in time for his son's basketball game. "He could be involved in the biggest deal that's going on, but nothing comes before his kids and his family," Paul says. Iger says it a topic they touch on a lot: "We talk about jettisoning anything else discretionary from your life except for work and family because there isn't room for anything else when you have a job like his or mine – you just can't go out and be with the guys very ofte

159

CHAPTER 12

'Leading for Innovation and Growth' Leadership Example: Fred Smith, Founder of FedEx

Following the translation of my book, *FedEx Delivers,* into Chinese, Russian, Spanish, Korean, Thai, Vietnamese, and several other languages, I often speak to business executives worldwide. The most common question is, "How did Fred Smith build such a great company?" People familiar with the history of FedEx may recall that the idea of a dedicated airline for express service was the subject of Fred's term paper at Yale. The development and implementation of this creative idea launched a company best described by this commercial,

"America, you've got a new airline! The first major airline in over 30 years, no first class, no meals, no movies, in fact, no passengers, just packages, small important shipments that have to get where they're going overnight ..."

FedEx is not an Overnight Success Story.

Like most startups, FedEx has had its share of problems. Many investors didn't think using a single city as a "hub" would work, and some doubted the need for an overnight delivery service altogether. During the first three years of its operations (1973-1975), FedEx lost over $29 million as it built its infrastructure and established the network that would allow it to start turning a profit.

On the inaugural night of operations in 1973, 389 FedEx employees and 14 Falcon jets delivered 186 packages overnight to 25 U.S. cities. Now, 50 years later, 600,000 team members and 697 aircraft deliver 16.5 million shipments daily for express, ground, freight, and expedited delivery services to more than 220 countries and territories, including every address in the United States. The Memphis hub, which started as a sorting table in a hangar, now occupies 900 acres with 200 miles of conveyors comprising a highly automated sorting system. One has to see it to appreciate how 10,000 people work together to unload, sort, and reload 200 planes every night in a highly tight operating window.

The Three Drivers Behind FedEx's Global Success Journey

- Relentless focus and pursuit of perfection in serving the customer
- Introduction and innovative application of technology
- PSP culture and leadership tapping employees' discretionary effort

Yes, Fred's original creative idea launched FedEx. Still, his genius is building the innovation and growth engine that powered FedEx during the early years and continues to do so fifty years later. Historically, companies become complacent and lose some of their competitive edge when they grow big. Still, this engine has kept FedEx's growth drivers front and center, the key to its sustained market leadership. FedEx has consistently ranked as one of the world's most admired companies and among the 100 best workplaces.

Continuous Innovation Engine Powering FedEx's Growth

Here are just a few innovations FedEx introduced over the past forty years.

- First express shipping company to own and operate aircraft, package sorting facilities, and delivery vans
- Launched COSMOS (Customer Operations Service Master Online System) - the information system FedEx uses to track every package and document they transport
- First express company to equip delivery vans with an electronic communication system, DADS (Digitally Assisted Dispatch System)
- The first company to introduce specialty packaging supplies to meet specific customer needs – such as the Overnight Letter and Courier Pak,
- First express company to offer delivery at 10:30 a.m.
- The first express company to introduce a PC-based automated shipping system
- Introduced SuperTracker, a hand-held barcode scanner system
- Development of an Integrated, Seamless International and Domestic Network
- The first company to offer online tracking by launching fedex.com

I was fortunate to join FedEx in the early days and be part of the management team that helped it become a global icon. As a member of the Long-Range Planning Committee (LRPC), I got to work closely with Fred and the senior management team and observe Fred's key role in designing the FedEx innovation and growth engine firsthand.

Great Strategy + Great Execution = Great Results

A lot has been written about Fred being a visionary and strategic thinker. All of that is true. But in addition to being a top-rate strategic mind, his attention to detail has been the key to the successful execution of FedEx's growth strategy. In FedEx's operations, every minute counts. Every day, each component of the global operations has to work like clockwork to deliver the absolutely positively overnight promise. One delayed flight from any city around the world can impact the whole system. I vividly remember meetings, lasting hours, where he would question us, the planning engineers, in detail about a single operational element.

Throughout this article, I'll use Fred's personal leadership examples to illustrate his deliberate planning and actions in building the FedEx innovation and growth engine. An organization's culture is set and reinforced by the day-to-day behavior of the founder and the senior management team during its early days. Managers and employees at all levels follow the senior management's example.

Five Components of the FedEx Innovation and Growth Engine (Model C4P)

1. Customer – The engine's core is customers. Everything, from strategy development to day-to-day execution, is driven by customer needs.

2. Purpose – Creating and keeping customers is the shared business purpose across the organization. Everyone clearly understands that FedEx creates and keeps customers by designing and delivering innovative logistics solutions and offering competitively superior customer value.

3. Process – Nothing happens in the business world without a process. The business purpose is realized through innovative, technology-enabled, and continually enhanced processes for designing and delivering superior customer value

4. People – It's people who execute these processes. FedEx people choosing to give the gift of their discretionary effort is the key to successfully executing business processes.

5. PSP Culture and Leadership – Why do FedEx people give the gift of their discretionary effort? FedEx successfully tapped into employees' discretionary effort because of its People Service Profit culture and the corresponding leadership practices.

Every business has these five components in some form. The unique thing about FedEx is how it has synergistically used these components to continually adapt its business model to changing customer needs and the larger business environment; how it has creatively used technology to enhance its customer value propositions and business processes; how it has updated its operational and leadership skill sets at every level to maintain market leadership and how it keeps innovating and outperforming the competition. The five components that constitute FedEx's Innovation and Growth engine were the keys to FedEx overcoming the many obstacles encountered during the early years. As reflected by the arrows around the growth engine diagram below, building and sustaining a great company is not a one-time project but an ongoing process.

1. Customer: Everybody's Line of Sight Focused on the Customer

The larger circle below represents FedEx – the entire organization – and the small circle at the center represents the customer.

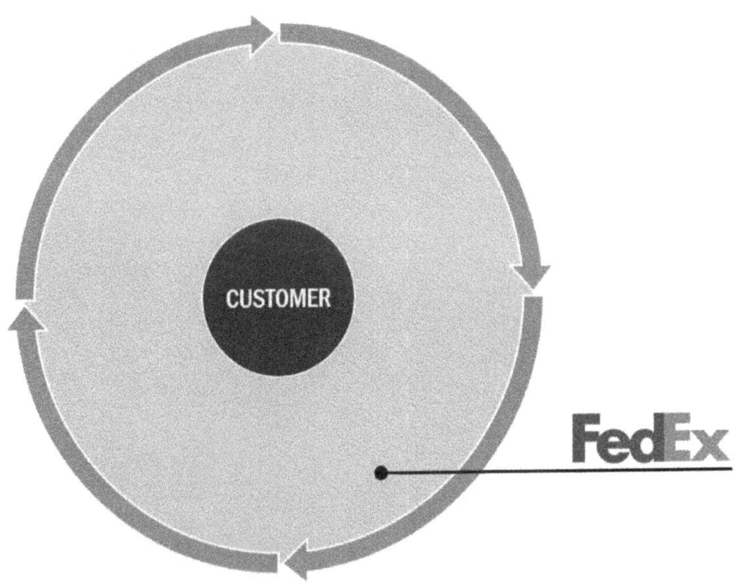

Figure 12.1

During the early years, it was common for Fred and other senior officers to stop by a department and talk to the employees. During one such stop in the Customer Service department, a customer service representative told Fred, "Mr. Smith, we're honored and privileged to work for you." Fred immediately responded, "You're wrong." Everyone gasped. "The truth is that I work for you. You're the first person the customer contacts when he wants to schedule a pick-up or has a question." Then, he drew the upside-down organization pyramid with customers on top, followed by direct customer contact employees and the CEO at the bottom. "You serve the customer, and all of us in management serve you." He repeatedly reiterated this 'Servant Leadership' model to groups throughout the organization. His goal was to ensure that everyone understood that you were serving the customer or someone who was. Visualize employees at the outer edge of the circle with their line of sight focused on the customer as they move their package to the final destination by handing it to the person next to them.

Figure 12.2

Relentless Pursuit of Perfection in serving the customer

From the early days, FedEx commercials successfully established top-of-mind awareness – "When it has to be there absolutely, positively overnight, think of FedEx." - To deliver on this promise, the expressed goal for every department was a 100% service level. Fred Smith personally chaired a global conference call every morning to review the previous day's performance. Every flight, maintenance, sort, and operational delay was analyzed in detail to identify its root cause and the corresponding corrective actions to ensure that it did not happen again. Fred's involvement communicated to everyone in the organization that anything less than 100% is unacceptable.

'Customer Needs' Dictating and Disrupting the Business Model

For some customers, FedEx's Priority Overnight service (which guaranteed delivery by 10:30 a.m. the next day) was too costly. They wanted overnight service but at a cheaper price. So, FedEx introduced a less expensive 'Standard Overnight Service' with guaranteed delivery the following afternoon. During the development and analysis of the new service, the Finance department objected, claiming that it would dilute the higher margin Priority Overnight business and thus negatively impact revenue and profits. Fred decided to go ahead anyway. Similar concerns were raised when we evaluated 'Ground Service,' a much cheaper option than air. Each time, Fred's message was that we've got to adapt our business model to what the customers want. He said that either we dilute the business ourselves or somebody else will do it for us. Today, the ground business and its profit contribution are growing much faster than air.

2. Shared Purpose: Create and Keep Customers

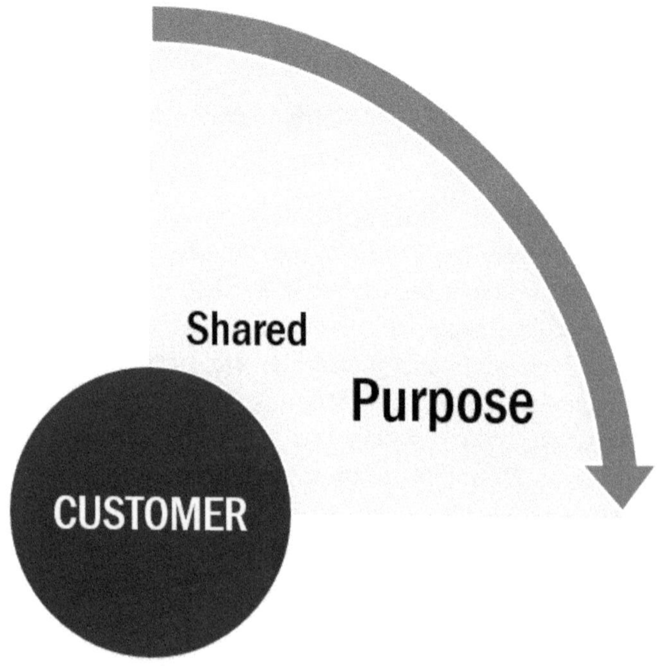

Figure 12.3

After moving into a management position at FedEx, every employee was required to attend a weeklong class at the FedEx Leadership Institute. There was a class for new front-line managers, new senior managers, and a class for new managing directors.

During the late 80s and early 90s, when FedEx was growing by leaps and bounds, Fred Smith and Jim Barksdale, the Chief Operating Officer, made it a point to address every class for new front-line managers. They wanted to make sure these new managers got off on the right foot, and they wanted to demonstrate their commitment to front-line employees and their managers, who, according to the company's culture and philosophy, are critically important to the company's success because they're closest to the customer. Each session with Fred and Jim was like a tag team match: first Fred, then Jim, or vice versa, depending on their schedules. Whenever it was Fred's turn, after earnestly welcoming the class to FedEx management and the special trust that entailed, he would ask, "What's the purpose of any business?"

Remember that FedEx promotes from within, so the class wasn't full of recently graduated MBAs from prestigious business schools. Most of them were former couriers picking up and delivering packages or men and women handling those packages at the hub or an airport ramp. They may have been agents helping customers on the phone or mechanics maintaining vehicles or jetliners. So, their answers were, in layman's terms, usually some variant of "to make a profit."

At that point, Fred - seemingly switching subjects - would ask, "Is the purpose of our lives to breathe?" After nervous laughter and quizzical looks from the class, he would answer his question. "Of course not. Each of us has our own purpose in life, depending on our values and goals, but we couldn't achieve those goals if we weren't breathing. From now on, I want you to think about making a profit like the way you think about breathing. Just as we have to breathe to go on living, we have to make a profit to keep the enterprise going, pay our salaries, buy the computers, vans, planes, and trucks we use, invest in future growth, and make sure shareholders get a return on their investment. But that's not our purpose. Our purpose, and the purpose of every business, is to create and keep customers. After all, they're the ones who generate the revenue that pays our bills, and if we run our business efficiently, yields the profit that we share at the end of the year."

Fred may have borrowed this customer-centric notion from Peter Drucker, but he still believes it with every fiber of his being. He used this initial question about a company's purpose as a kick-off point to ensure all new managers focused more than anything else on serving customers. If they weren't serving customers directly, Fred wanted them to be serving those employees who were serving customers. He wanted - and to this day still wants - to make sure that at every point of contact with FedEx, each customer has a positive experience. At the end of the day, we're achieving 100% customer satisfaction or as close to that as humanly possible.

"A satisfied customer made this possible."

This phrase was printed on the front of FedEx paycheck envelopes to remind all employees that satisfying the customer is everyone's responsibility. It made the goal clear: 100 percent customer satisfaction after every interaction and transaction and 100 percent service performance, ensuring that all deliveries are made within the time commitment for the service selected by the customer.

To keep FedEx's customer satisfaction level at 100%, the overall customer service measurement included 12 critical points in the value chain, highlighting the elements of service that the customers value. The 12 elements helped various departments and employees see which part of the value chain their work directly affected. Measuring these elements helped employees see their performance against the 100% customer satisfaction goal. This comprehensive measure of overall customer satisfaction and service quality is called Service Quality Indicator (SQI). There was a report card on the previous day's performance every morning. SQI translates the customer value proposition into measurable goals.

From A Functional to Customer Orientation

This shared purpose helped employees move from a functional orientation to a customer or business orientation. Instead of thinking, "I did my job," employees were encouraged to think about the customer, i.e., making sure they, their department and ultimately the company, FedEx, delivered on its promise.

The call from a prominent medical laboratory in Phoenix was urgent. Shipments of amniotic fluid from two high-risk pregnancies had failed to arrive for testing. If they didn't come soon, the mothers-to-be would have to endure the difficult procedure again. Senior customer representative Brenda Curry got on the phone and found the shipments on a truck near Dallas. With help from FedEx operations staff, she had the truck stopped and 20,000 pounds of freight unloaded to retrieve the two samples. "Get them to Phoenix, and I'll take care of them," Curry told the Dallas ramp manager. She met the flight carrying the shipments at 11 p.m., stored them in her refrigerator as instructed by the lab, and delivered them personally the next day. "Why did you do this?" asked the laboratory technician. "It needed to be done," Curry replied, "and I was there." Three days later, the laboratory called to let Curry know that her efforts had paid off. The samples were just fine. This is just one of the hundreds of experiences that take place regularly around the FedEx global network.

FedEx achieves its shared purpose of creating and keeping customers by designing and delivering innovative logistics solutions, a competitively superior customer value proposition. Nothing happens in the business world without a process. FedEx has well-thought-out processes for designing the customer value proposition elements and delivering them consistently day in and day out. In FedEx operations, every minute counts. Innovative application of technology has been, and continues to play, a crucial role in FedEx's operations and business processes.

3. Technology Enabled Processes for Creating and Keeping Customers

Fred Smith has single-handedly changed the way global business functions. He has achieved this transformation not because he happened to be in the right place at the right time or because he had access to new groundbreaking technology but because he had a vision of combining existing technologies and developing new processes to realize new possibilities.

Strategy & Leadership, September/October 1997

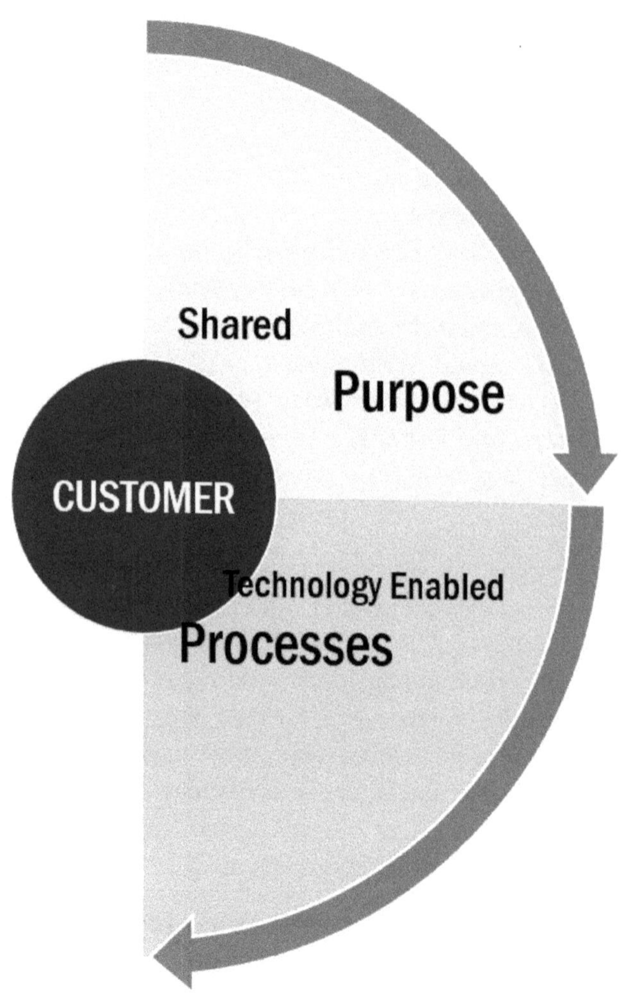

Figure 12.4

During the last three years of my 22-year career at FedEx, I facilitated week-long leadership development classes in the company's Leadership Institute for all levels of management. I'd take the class to his conference room to meet Fred's request to interact with the new managing directors. In a typical appearance, he would talk about the company's strategy and the critical role managing directors play in executing it. Then, he would stay as long as needed to answer questions. In one class, a participant asked, "Mr. Smith, when you look back at your legacy, what will you be most proud of?" He thought briefly, then answered, "Introducing technology in the logistics business."

Technology-Driven Solutions to Meet Customers' 'Peace of Mind' Needs

While FedEx was founded on the idea of meeting time-definite express transportation needs, the business really took off when Fred Smith realized that the company was not in the transportation business but in the 'peace of mind' business. He said, "The information about the package is as important as the package." The new business purpose resulted in the development and implementation of innovative electronic package tracking systems designed to let customers know exactly where their packages were at any given time, including when they had arrived at their final destinations.

This innovation required much more than applying existing technologies. Hundreds of information technologists had to create new hardware and software solutions that employees throughout the organization would have to implement flawlessly. The successful implementation of the expanding business models required innovative (what-if) thinking across the organization.

The "What-if" Culture Turning One Technology Innovation into Four

FedEx is big on acronyms. Each package is assigned an alpha-numeric code, a URSA (Universal Routing and Sort Aid) code for routing and sorting packages, determined by its origin and destination zip codes. In the early days, when a courier would pick up a package, she would look up the codes in a printed courier guide and then write them on the package using a marker. So there was always a chance that the courier might transpose digits, and the package would be misrouted. Since the new electronic tracking system already included the origin and destination zip codes, people in the field picking up the boxes began to ask, "What if our trackers print the URSA codes on labels that we could then just stick on packages?" At that time in the U.S., there were no portable printers that a courier could hang on his shoulder and print the URSA label. So, FedEx worked with vendors and developed a portable printer.

Once couriers could generate printed URSA labels on the fly, folks at the Hub responsible for sorting and routing packages to their final destinations began to ask, "What if you print the URSA in a barcode format? That would enable us to automate the sorting process." It didn't take long before we started printing URSA barcodes, and as predicted, the automation substantially increased the Memphis hub's sorting capacity with minimal capital expenditure.

This cascade of innovations continued at the destination end of the business where employees responsible for delivering packages in the destination city observed that the tracking system had all the information about the packages due to arrive in our stations the following day and asked, "What if we used this information to plan delivery routes before the packages arrived?" That led to the development of more balanced delivery routes, which led to more efficient use of resources and further ensured on-time deliveries.

Automation of Hub Sort Operations: Using Technology to Create Time

The Memphis super hub connects every point in FedEx's network. Even a slight delay could impact the on-time delivery service levels the following day worldwide. Nevertheless, some delays can't be avoided. The weather may prevent flights from taking off or landing on time. Air traffic controllers might hold up flights for any number of reasons. Unanticipated maintenance problems are bound to crop up every once in a while. So, they are bound to have a few late arriving flights every night. In the early days, the system could accommodate a certain number of late inbound flights and still launch the outbound flights on time. But as the business grew, there needed to be more play in the system to accommodate late arriving flights without affecting the launch time of outbound flights.

Here's one way FedEx, in effect, gained more time to launch outbound flights. Every plane contains three different types of shipments – small packages and letters, boxes, and palletized freight. Loading those shipments onto an aircraft takes a certain amount of processing time. Early on, shipments were processed sequentially regardless of their category. Eventually, however, an automated Small Package Sort System (SPSS), essentially a hub within a hub, was proposed to the senior management. It would enable the different types of shipments to be processed in parallel rather than sequentially. Even though the labor savings generated from the proposed change were insufficient to justify the multi-million-dollar capital expenditure, Fred approved the project because it allowed the Hub to finish the sort and launch planes on time so customers would get their shipments when expected.

FedEx is in the business of delivering packages on time every day. The average customer does not care whether it has been delivering on time for the past six months; he cares whether FedEx can deliver his shipment on time today. From pickup to sorting, to flying, to customs clearance, to delivery, the entire organization worldwide has to work as one team to meet customers' needs and expectations flawlessly day after day. On a given day, there might be snow in Chicago, a traffic jam in the Lincoln Tunnel in New York, or problems with the customs system in Mumbai. FedEx people choosing to give the gift of their discretionary effort – commitment and creativity – are the key to successfully executing these processes in normal and adverse conditions.

4. People's Discretionary Effort: The Key to Flawless Process Execution

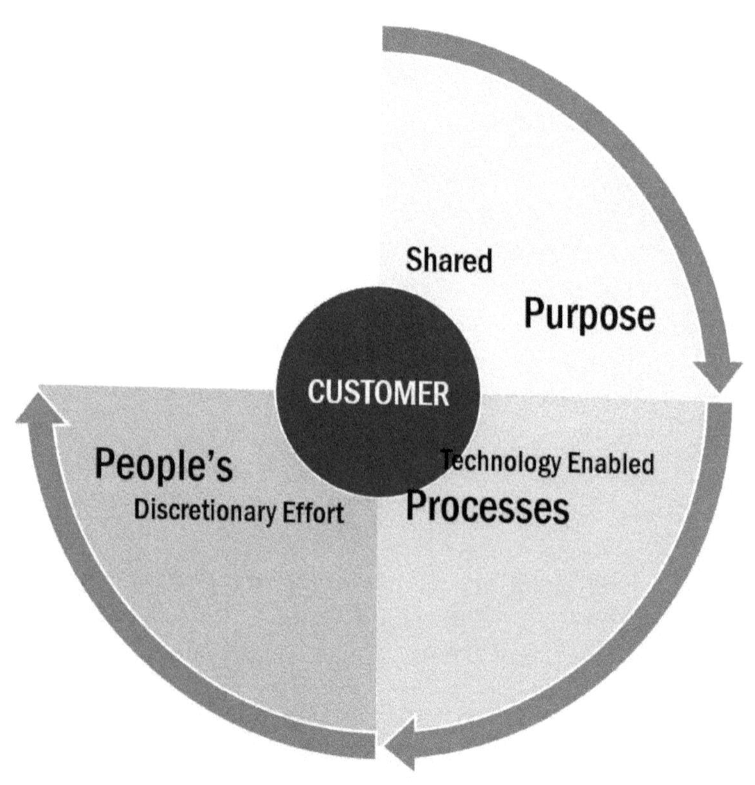

Figure 12.5

'Whatever it Takes' Commitment

This commitment to the goal of 100 percent customer satisfaction drives FedEx people around the globe to go above and beyond. In Omaha, Nebraska, ramp agents swarm to the plane to help handlers roll containers out of the upper deck. On a busy morning at Narita airport in Tokyo, a ramp manager helps unload boxes onto a conveyor belt. A courier in Louisiana wades through flooded streets to deliver payroll to a customer. In rural Texas, a courier has made a point of recognizing his customers' cars so he can flag them down for a delivery. In Ho Chi Minh City, a courier hops off his moped when he can't get through a crowded Vietnamese market and delivers his packages on foot.

Taking Initiative to Generate and Implement Creative Ideas

FedEx started by delivering packages only Monday through Friday. On customers' request, FedEx began offering a Saturday delivery option. On Fridays, when a customer called to arrange pickup, the customer service agent on the phone asked, "Would you like the shipment to be delivered Saturday for an extra $10?" This question would lead to a delay while the customer checked whether they wanted a Saturday delivery. A manager in the Boston Call Center noticed the time customer service agents had to wait while the customers who called to schedule pickups put calls on hold and checked about the Saturday delivery option with others at their offices. It was not a smooth experience for the customer either. The call center manager suggested changing the question to a statement: "If you would like a Saturday delivery, please mark the airway bill accordingly. There will be a $10 surcharge. Otherwise, the package will be delivered on Monday." The call was complete, and the wait time was eliminated for the customer and the agent. The customer had all the information they needed to make the appropriate decision before the courier arrived to collect the package.

Implementing this simple idea in all call centers resulted in vastly improved customer experience, increased agent productivity, and significant cost savings.

Serving Customers during the Olympics

Australia was gearing up for the 2000 Summer Olympics. The traffic restrictions in Sydney would shut FedEx's pickup and delivery operations down. There would be no parking on the streets during regular delivery hours. The FedEx team in Australia tackled this challenge by sending a questionnaire out to customers, asking if they would be open. If they were going to be open, the questionnaire asked when and how FedEx could serve their needs during the Olympics. Some customers were planning on opening earlier so they could receive deliveries then. For the rest, the team devised a plan to have multiple couriers in one vehicle. FedEx delivery trucks would circle the area, and the extra couriers would deliver the packages while the trucks kept moving. FedEx customers were delighted!

Why do FedEx employees choose to give the gift of their discretionary effort? The final component of the innovation and growth engine provides the answer.

5. PSP Culture and Leadership

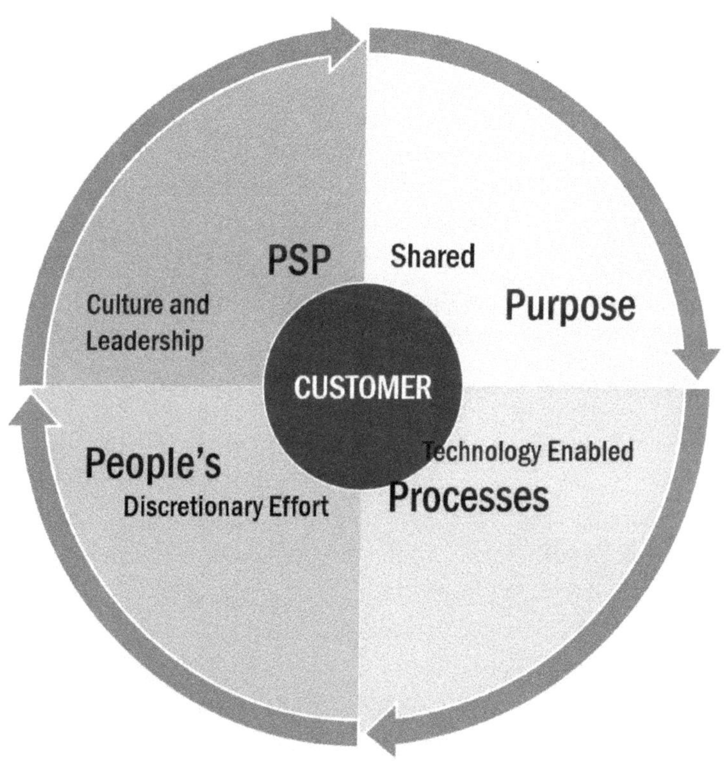

Figure 12.6

PSP Culture was integral to Fred's business plan for starting FedEx. In my first week at FedEx, I attended an all-day orientation session conducted by the human resources department. The human resources manager talked a lot about FedEx's PSP culture, which stands for 'People, Service, Profit,' and its 'People First' philosophy. Put simply, the PSP culture means that FedEx puts its people (employees) first in everything it does, and as a result, FedEx employees put the customer first in everything they do.

Another metaphor used to explain the PSP culture was a three-legged stool. Each of the three legs is equally important. And each leg must be equally strong for the stool to be stable. For FedEx to be healthy and strong, all three elements of the PSP culture had to be strong. If you treat people well, they will be more inclined to provide excellent service, which will generate profits that benefit everyone.

My department was responsible for developing long-range operations and facilities plans for FedEx locations worldwide. I rode with couriers in Tokyo, Hong Kong, Bombay, and several other cities. My experience riding with Susan – observing the mutually respectful interaction between the customers and the couriers – confirmed for me the crucial role of the PSP culture and the "People First" philosophy as a critical element that helped FedEx define the industry standard for customer service and reliability. In my twenty-two years at FedEx, while on business trips, whenever possible, I set aside at least half a day for riding with a courier in the city. I found this to be the best way to get a feel for the unique characteristics of that market and the local operating scenario. I observed the same above-and-beyond dedication in employees in every city and country. Leading people, ' the FedEx Way,' produced similar results worldwide.

An employee gives this gift of commitment when the leader, through their day-to-day behaviors, makes the employee **feel** that:

- I'm making a difference

- I'm part of a winning team that's going somewhere

- The leader cares about me as a person and is meeting my needs to:

  - be challenged and grow professionally
  - be appreciated when I go above and beyond
  - be listened to when I have ideas to share

Leading for Innovation Leadership Practices

In every communication, Fred and the senior management team reminded employees: "Every package they handle is a golden package. It might be someone's mortgage payment or a lifesaving article. It may be a birthday present from grandparents for their grandchild. It may be a critical spare part needed to fix a downed assembly line. You're making a difference every day!"

Several years after I left FedEx, I visited the FedEx headquarters to exercise some options to get more FedEx stock. I was in the elevator when Fred Smith, founder and CEO of FedEx, stepped in.

He asked, "Madan, how are you doing?"

"Fine, sir," I responded.

Wanting to make small talk, I said, "Fred, I saw you at the Tigers (University of Memphis' Basketball team) game last week."

"Yes, I go to some games." He replied.

"Fred, I need to thank you."

"For what?" he asked.

"The only thing doing well in my portfolio is FedEx stock. Everything else has been going down."

"Madan, you need to have confidence in FedEx stock. You helped design the system."

"Fred, I absolutely do, and that's why I'll be holding on to the FedEx stock."

The elevator reached the ground floor; we shook hands and walked out to our respective cars.

Even though I'd been gone from FedEx for several years, Fred still made a point to remind me that I made a difference, exhibiting a fundamental leadership behavior for tapping into employees' creativity and commitment. Leading by example, Fred inspired all FedEx managers to lead for innovation and growth.

A Handwritten Note from the CEO

A story related to me by Gloria Sangster-Fort from her experience in FedEx's Sales department is an excellent example of commitment in action. FedEx was starting to offer international express service. She approached a Fortune 100 company that was international in scope for handling their international shipments. They asked for a reference. At that time, FedEx did not have any big clients shipping internationally.

Gloria was talking to Frank Newman, a colleague at FedEx, about her dilemma in trying to sign up this rather large account for FedEx's international service. Frank was not part of the Sales organization but was familiar with writing operational plans and working internationally from previous experience. He volunteered to help her develop a proposal. He mapped the process and developed a detailed plan, a FedEx solution to handle the business in the three targeted European countries. This plan showed how FedEx would streamline the shipping process and substantially improve the service.

It took Frank two weeks of dedicated effort to develop this comprehensive proposal. Frank had no stake, direct responsibility, or personal gain from getting this customer's international business. But he was committed to FedEx and was willing to do whatever it took to help FedEx grow. This proposal made Gloria secure the account and the first ever $10M contract. Sales awarded him a handsome Bravo Zulu letter and check to show their appreciation for this above-and-beyond effort. The letter was retained and displayed. Based on this successful experience, Sales created a model for use in working with other large companies.

Frank was never forgotten for his "above and beyond work." In fact, he was later hired into sales and became a managing director. Frank had become known for being innovative and customer-centric because of a deed that he did not 'have to' perform. Gloria had received many awards during her twenty-year career at FedEx. Still, she cherishes the most a brief handwritten note from Fred Smith after she secured DuPont's international business. It was common to see Fred or Jim's handwritten, framed notes in people's offices and cubicles.

Fred Willing to Be Challenged and Change His Mind

Graham Smith, Vice President of Properties at FedEx, shared the following story that illustrates a vital quality of an innovation leader - the willingness to be challenged and change his mind. "Since the inception of operations at the Memphis International Airport, FedEx enjoyed an excellent working relationship with the 164th Airlift Wing of the Tennessee Air National Guard (TN ANG), which occupied 103 acres of leased property contiguous to the FedEx hub. Over the years, quite a number of proposals were advanced to relocate the Guard and make their land and facilities available to accommodate FedEx's growth. After much serious analysis and discussion, a 'final' decision was reached early in the new millennium that such an option was not in FedEx's best interest.

Some nine months later, the US Air Force developed a change of mission for the 164th, which would require millions in renovation costs to the existing site. FedEx Properties, the Airport Authority, and TN ANG then developed a tri-party proposal wherein FedEx would contribute funds, which, combined with the renovation costs authorized by the Air Force, would allow the TN ANG to relocate to a green field site. TN ANG would enjoy a newly designed facility, the airport authority could start developing the east perimeter of the airport, and FedEx would step into a long-term lease at virtually no cost beyond the funds contributed.

Having recently been instructed to terminate further consideration of the TN ANG site, I was reluctant to engage Fred in conversation about another proposal! Instead of summarily dismissing my initial call, he immediately and actively engaged in a detailed discussion of all aspects of the proposal made some excellent suggestions, expressed genuine appreciation for the creative solution, and encouraged me to immediately and actively pursue the proposal with all parties. By his willingness to re-look at new concepts and offer active support along the way, he provided the visionary leadership that assured the success of what, in hindsight, became one of the most important strategic facility acquisitions since the Company began operations."

The captain needs co-pilots for the airplane to fly long distances and soar to new heights. Leading by example, Fred has developed a management team that is taking FedEx to new heights. You see 'Leading for Innovation and Growth' leadership practices in action daily at all management levels.

A Telephone Call from the COO, one of the co-pilots, is just one such example

During my career at FedEx, I received several awards, but the ones I remember and cherish the most did not involve plaques or checks. They were heartfelt phone calls and notes. One of those phone calls involved my small part in helping FedEx become the first service company to win the Malcolm Baldrige Quality Award in 1990. As part of the evaluation process, the examiners interviewed me about the strategic planning process at FedEx. I spent three hours doing my best to answer their questions.

I was a little nervous when Jim Barksdale, Chief Operating Officer, called me the following day. The night before, the examiners had briefed the executive management about their interviews that day. To my surprise and relief, Jim said they were very impressed by the strategic planning process I described. He thanked me "for doing such a good job." This brief phone call made me feel great for weeks. The fact that Jim had made a mental note of my contribution during the briefing and had taken the time from his busy schedule to call me first thing in the morning spoke volumes. I felt in my heart that Jim cared about my contribution and me.

The following statement by Fred after FedEx has been in operation for thirty-five years summarizes the critical role of co-pilots, "But I also say, I'm proud to be part of a team that focuses on the future and new ways we can help our customers achieve their goals in the vast marketplace. In fact, I often tell people that FedEx is just getting started." FedEx's journey to becoming a global icon shows that when customer focus, technology, people, and innovative leadership come together, an organization can scale new heights.

Throughout our careers, we all work with and for many leaders. There are some leaders we admire and wish to gain some of their leadership traits, and some do not, hoping never to be like them. I was fortunate to work with great leaders like Fred Smith and Jim Barksdale at FedEx. They taught me that '*Leading for Innovation and Growth*' requires two distinct skill sets:

1. People skills: to tap into people's discretionary effort, their creativity, and commitment.
2. Innovative business thinking: to develop and implement growth strategies informed by changes in the larger environment.

For sustained growth in the 21st century, the '*Leading for Innovation and Growth*' style of leadership is needed at all levels of an organization. This critical business need presents an excellent opportunity to make a difference and enjoy a successful career. Growing as a professional, a leader, and a human being is a lifelong journey rather than a singular destination. I hope the knowledge shared in this book helps you enjoy this incredible journey and celebrate life in its fullness.

Acknowledgements

In addition to spending time with family and friends and playing golf, I enjoy being on college campuses as a guest speaker. COVID put a stop to all in-person speaking. I tried guest speaking via Zoom but found the experience not as enjoyable. Because of the lack of in-person exchange of ideas, the source of intellectual stimulation. I had to do something to fill this intellectual stimulation gap. That's when the idea of starting another book came to mind. I love the whole process of writing a book – reading for research, interviewing people, thinking conceptually, and putting thoughts on paper. The serendipity of running into the appropriate material for the chapter I am in the middle of.

My first step in starting a book is to get feedback on the book's subject from a sample of the target audience. I emailed a four-page document on the book topic to successful and proven leaders whose opinions I value and respect. I want to thank Matt Holt, Jay Myers, James Lewellen, Graham Smith, Ben Buffington, Ian Birla, Amit Maheshwari, and Rob Carter for taking the time to read the document and provide feedback and encouragement to proceed.

Next, I want to thank Achint, the most helpful person throughout the book-writing process. He not only edited each chapter and designed the graphics but also shared practical suggestions for conveying the message more clearly. The book would not have been possible without his ongoing support and help.

I want to thank Gary Bronson, Reinhard Fischer, Allen Darnell, and Rob Carter for making time on their busy calendars to share the details of their journey from technical professionals to innovation leaders.

I want to thank Duke, University of Memphis, Christian Brothers University, and other colleges for allowing me to discuss and get feedback on the material with their computer science and engineering graduate students. The feedback based on their real-world experience has significantly helped refine the material.

Finally, I want to convey my most profound appreciation to Shashi, my life partner, for allowing me to spend hours in the study working on this book.

About the Author

Author (left) receiving Five Star Awards, the highest recognition for Leadership Excellence at FedEx, from Fred Smith, Founder and CEO of FedEx.

Madan Birla is a veteran of the "hard" side of business. In his 22 years at FedEx, he worked closely with Fred Smith (founder and CEO) and the senior management team in evaluating strategic "what-ifs."

His life experiences in two rich cultures, East and West, and his broad educational background have prepared him to creatively meld ideas from engineering, business, and psychology to develop comprehensive "Leading for Innovation and Growth" models.

After completing undergraduate work in Mechanical Engineering at BITS-Pilani, India, he received his Master of Science in industrial engineering from the Illinois Institute of Technology (IIT) in Chicago, Illinois. After graduating from IIT, he joined RCA in Indianapolis. While in Indianapolis, he did graduate work in business at Butler University. After moving to Memphis to join FedEx, he received a Master of Science in counseling from the University of Memphis. He has been inducted into Alpha Pi Mu, Honor Society for Industrial Engineers, and the University of Memphis' College of Education's Alumni Hall of Fame. He serves on the dean's advisory council.

He regularly speaks in executive education programs at Kellogg Management Institute, Northwestern, Tuck Business School, Dartmouth, Columbia, Duke, University of Miami, American Management Association, The Conference Board, Indian School of Business, Indian Institute of Management, and Singapore Institute of Management.

He regularly speaks at businesses worldwide, including Google, IBM, Microsoft, Bridgestone, Smith & Nephew, SONY, Tata Consultancy Services, Infosys, Hilton, Marriott, and others.

For giving back to the community, he works regularly with non-profit boards and management teams to help develop strategic plans, including Wings Cancer Foundation, Literacy Mid-South, Church Health Center, Friends for Life, Tipton County Commission on Aging, Collierville School System, and others.

His book, *FedEx Delivers: How the World's Leading Shipping Company Keeps Innovating and Outperforming the Competition,* published by John Wiley & Sons, has been translated into Orthodox Chinese, Simplified Chinese, Russian, Spanish, Korean, Vietnamese, Thai, Arabic, and other languages. His other books are *Balanced Life and Leadership Excellence: A Nurturing Relationship,* translated into German; *Unleashing Creativity and Innovation: Nine Lessons from Nature for Enterprise Growth and Career Success;* and *Enjoy Balance and Unleash Creativity: Five Steps to a Happier, Healthier and Successful Life.*

Bibliography

Anne, commenting on a column, The New York Times, May 13, 2016

Birla, Madan, *FedEx Delivers,* John Wiley & Sons, New York, 2005

Birla, Madan, *Unleashing Creativity and Innovation,* John Wiley & Sons, New York, 2014

Birla, Madan, *Enjoy Balance and Unleash Creativity,* Vishwakarma Publications, Pune, 2016

Bennis, Warren & Nanus, Bert, *Leaders,* Harper & Row, ew York, 1985

Cribbin, James, *Leadership Strategies for Organizational Effectiveness,* AMACOM, New York, 1981

Bloomberg Businessweek, April 14, 2022, May 16, 2022, August 2, 2022

Bryant, Adam, The New York Times, Corner Office interview,

Bryant, Adam, *Google's Quest to Build Better Boss,* The New York Times, 2011

Cook, Tim, *University of Naples, Commencement Address,* 2023

Ellis, Lindsay, The Wall Street Journal, February 14, 2022

Florez, Gregory, Real Simple Magazine, May 2011

Gates, Bill, *Business @The Speed of Thought,* Warner Books, Inc., New York 1999

Gerstner, Louis, IBM Annual Report, 1993

Gore, Mike, Team Trek Newsletter, 2023

Greenleaf, Robert, *Servant Leadership,* Paulist Press, Mahwah, NJ 1977

Jobs, Steve, Stanford University, Commencement Address, June 12, 2005

Kruger, Pamela, Fast Company Magazine, June 1999

Lamarre, Daniel, Bloomberg Businessweek, 2023

Lee, Blain, *The Power of Principle: Influence with Honor,* Fireside, New York 1998

Lynch, Karen, Bloomberg Businessweek, 2020

Malesic, Jonathan, The New York Times, January 3, 2023

Management Review, November 1998

Mather, John, TIME 100, June 2022

Mehta, Apoorva, Instacart Founder, FORTUNE, October 1, 2015

Moss Kanter, Rosabeth*, The Change Masters, Simon & Schuster, New York 1985*

Nadella, Satya, *Hit Refresh,* written with Greg Shaw and Jill Tracie Nichols, Harper Collins, New York, 2017

Nagle, Bernhard and Pascarella, Perry, *Leveraging People and Profit: The Hard Work of Soft Management,* Butterworth – Heinemann, New York 1998

Newton, James, *Uncommon Friends,* Harcourt Brace, San Diego 1987

Paul Chris, Bloomberg Businessweek, April 14, 2022

Pink, Daniel, *A Whole New Mind, Riverhead Book, New York 2005*

Pearson, Carol, *The Hero Within: Six Archetypes We Live By,* Harper One, San Francisco, 2015

Powell Jobs, Laurene, TIME 100, June 13, 2022

Powell, John, *Why Am I Afraid to Tell You Who I am?* Tabor Publishing, Valencia 1969

Rabinowicz, Anna, O magazine, February 2011

Robinson, Alan, *Corporate Creativity,* Barrett-Koehler, Oakland, CA 1998

Schmidt, Eric & Jonathan Rosenberg, *How Google Works,* Grand Central Publishing, a division of Hachette Book Group, New York, 2014

Simmons, Mary, FORTUNE, August 17, 2009

Singh, Harmit, Levi's CFO, Bloomberg Businessweek

Slok, Carolyn, Science of Mind magazine

Smith, Brad, Intuit CEO, Fast Company magazine

Strategy & Leadership magazine, Sept/Oct 1997

Tugend, Alia, The New York Times, March 20, 2015

www.ingramcontent.com/pod-product-compliance
Lightning Source LLC
Chambersburg PA
CBHW040755120726
48005CB00012B/1178